T0368371

Life Explained in 5 Easy Lessons:

A Spiritual Survival Guide for the End of the World

M ATTHEW L. W ILLIAMS

authorHOUSE

AuthorHouse™
1663 Liberty Drive
Bloomington, IN 47403
www.authorhouse.com
Phone: 833-262-8899

Published by AuthorHouse 10/30/2024

ISBN: 979-8-8230-3711-2 (sc)
ISBN: 979-8-8230-3710-5 (e)

Library of Congress Control Number: 2024923386

Contents

Contents

Lesson #1

Where Do We Go After Death?

Our life on earth is but a tiny blip in time when compared with the vast backdrop of endless eternity. Anyone can die suddenly and then be locked into an afterlife they don't want. Shouldn't we spend a little more time in this life preparing for the next, much longer one? Indeed, by comparing this very brief life with the much longer afterlife, we might even conclude—from length alone—that <u>the whole purpose</u> of this life is to secure the <u>best possible position</u> for ourselves in the eternal afterlife.

Of all living beings, <u>only people</u> have to worry about where they will spend eternity. This is because only people have an awareness of God and good and evil. Therefore we are accountable before God for all our actions in life.

All other creatures are lower life forms that lack spiritual awareness and a knowledge of God. They **pass at death directly to paradise in God's presence. Since they have no moral awareness of good and evil, God does not charge them with any sin. Being sinless, they are free to enter God's presence in heaven at death.**

St. Paul in *Romans* 5:13 explains the connection between sin and awareness of God's law of right and wrong,

> "To be sure, sin was in the world before the
> law was given, but **sin is not charged
> against anyone's account where there is no law.**"

Paul expresses this idea even more succinctly in *Romans* 4:15,

> "Where there is no law, there is no sin."

1

God here is applying a **relative** standard of judgement. That is, he judges us relative to or <u>proportionate</u> to how much moral awareness we possess. That is, did we know an action was right or wrong when we did it? An **absolute** standard of justice is much harsher. In an absolute system, God will judge you for doing something wrong even if you <u>didn't</u> know it was wrong when you did it. More on this later.

How Do We Know that Animals—And All Lower Life Forms—Go to Heaven?

The Bible often uses metaphors or word pictures to convey truth. The Garden of Eden in *Genesis* is a metaphor for heaven. All of God's creation—people <u>and</u> animals—dwell there in the Paradise of God's presence **because there is <u>no sin</u>**. Once Adam and Eve sin, they have to leave Eden—but the animals remain because they <u>never sinned</u> since they lack moral awareness. **Just as the animals were with God in Eden, they will be with him in heaven**.

Noah's Ark is another metaphor that is relevant. It teaches us that God will destroy the wicked, but save the righteous. All those on the Ark—Noah's family <u>and</u> the animals—are deemed righteous. They are spared God's judgement and will be able to dwell with Him in Heaven when they die.

Metaphors aside, **people who deny that animals go to heaven—don't realize they are effectively <u>accusing God of creating an unjust world</u>. They are thereby implying that <u>God himself</u> is unjust for doing so**. How so? Animals—like people—are brought into this world without their prior consent. They are just born into it. Bad things happen—like animals getting torn to pieces by a predator. If there is no other dimension—such as an afterlife— for animals, what do we say about a young animal, just born, that immediately gets torn to pieces and killed by a predator? That God brought it into this world just to cause it to suffer and die? This is slander against God.

The rule about evil in this world is twofold:

1. It occurs because it is <u>deserved</u> **for some earlier deed or offense**.

OR

2. It is **part of God's broad agenda** (= part of a jigsaw puzzle involving many billions and trillions of people and events **too large, complex and detailed for us to understand**). Actually, the numbers involved are much greater than mere billions and trillions. I merely use them as 'familiar' big numbers for us. But—**if the reason for evil is that it serves God's overall agenda—God compensates the victim with some <u>greater good</u>**.

Normally, this involves giving the victims of evil a blissful place in heaven for eternity. But **if animals don't go to heaven, then there is <u>no possible greater compensation</u>**. Or <u>any</u> compensation at all in the case of an animal killed at birth. God didn't bring the animal back to life with a higher status or prevent the trauma in the first place.

We are left to believe—under this scenario—that God brings innocent creatures into the world to suffer brutal atrocities and then die. There is **no way the Bible can be twisted or distorted to such a degree to support this idea**.

The standard God uses to judge animals—<u>also</u> applies to all human beings who lack moral awareness. For example, fetuses that die before birth, babies, very young children or those that are severely impaired—either mentally or in terms of their sanity.

For most people—who <u>do</u> possess moral awareness of their actions—their standing in the afterlife will be very <u>different</u> from that of animals and babies. The average person will <u>not</u> make it to paradise with God after death.

So where will people go when they die? One of three places:

1.) 'Living' Heaven (= Paradise)   about 17%
2.) 'Dead' Heaven   (= extinction of awareness) about 77%
3.) Hell   (= place of torment)   about 6%

What I call **Living Heaven** here is the same thing that I have elsewhere called Paradise. It is **a place of bliss (in God's Presence) in varying degrees**—in keeping with our earthly goodness when alive. It is what we typically think of when we picture heaven.

What I call **Dead Heaven** is an extinction of the senses so that you have no awareness or perception of anything because **God has put your—normally eternal—soul to death as a punishment for your shortcomings during your life on earth. It is a middle state in-between heaven and hell**. You are not rewarded with bliss as in heaven. Nor do you suffer torment as in hell. You simply cease to exist—just as you didn't exist before you were born. This is God's punishment for lukewarm believers as described in *Revelation* 3:16:

> "Because you are lukewarm—neither hot nor cold—I
> am about to spit you out of my mouth."

Some (misguided) people may feel happy that they could indulge in some earthly sin and only be sent to Dead Heaven—and not Hell itself. But at some point before God destroys their soul, they will feel the horror—not at going to hell, but at realizing they have lost out on going to heaven forever. That too is a form of horror—at Paradise lost.

Hell is the place of torment for those who have rejected God and refused his free gift of salvation. It—like heaven—has varying degrees. But the degrees of Hell are for the most hardened practitioners of evil. **Do not end up there—either by choice or out of ignorance.**

Jesus in *Matthew* 7:13-14 warns us that only a <u>few</u> will actually make it to Living Heaven,

"Enter through the narrow gate. For wide is the gate and broad is the road that leads to destruction, and many enter through it. But small is the gate and narrow the road that leads to life, and only a few find it."

The **'road that leads to life' refers to** reaching **Living Heaven** or Paradise in God's presence. Only a few—**1 in 6**—will actually manage to travel down it. The **'road that leads to destruction' refers to Dead Heaven and Hell combined** and—sadly—**5 out of 6** people will spiritually walk down this path during their life.

In Dead Heaven, God puts to death your eternal soul, while in Hell your soul is continuously tortured for eternity. Either way, your soul is destroyed—since God <u>designed</u> your soul to live forever and find peace and rest in his presence.

How Can We Possibly Know How Many People Go Where in the Afterlife?

This is a good question and one that should be asked. But **the answer is in the Bible** if you know where to look. For this, we must look to the ancient nation of Israel for guidance.

The **12 Tribes of ancient Israel** were known in the Bible as the 'Chosen People' of God. They **symbolize all people—from all times and places—who would one day become saved** and able to dwell with God at their death in Heaven. One of the reasons **God blessed ancient Israel** is **because their history—by God's deliberate design—illustrates spiritual principles that can teach the world**:

"I will make you a light to the nations—so
that all the world may be saved"
(*Isaiah* 49:6)

5

The **history of ancient Israel symbolizes God's salvation process for <u>all</u> mankind**. God first delivers the oppressed Israelites from the **'iron furnace' of ancient Egypt** (*Deuteronomy 4:20*)—which **symbolizes Hell**. They then wander in the wilderness until God brings them to the **Promised Land of Israel** which **symbolizes heaven**.

The Israelites then split into two groups. 10 of the 12 tribes are expelled from the land of Israel because of their sins—never to return. This group symbolizes the **majority of mankind** (= about 83%) that **will go to Dead Heaven** in the afterlife. The remaining 2 tribes are briefly expelled from the Promised Land—again, because of their sins. But they do manage to later return to Israel. So in the end they manage to stay in the Land. This group symbolizes those **few people** who **will make it to Living Heaven** (2 of 12 = 1 of 6 = **about 17%**).

While the Israelites were wandering in the wilderness on their way to the Promised Land, **God had to put to death a number of them**—for rebellion against him and other sin. These people—**about 6%** or so—**symbolize those people God will send to Hell**. We may subtract these 6% of hell-bound people from the less spiritual 83% of Israelites who were permanently kicked out of the Promised Land.

Historical Error

In the past, people assumed there were only <u>two</u> destinations for a person's soul after death—Heaven or Hell. Since Jesus told us only a few would find life in the afterworld, people assumed all the rest were going to Hell. They believed the fallacy that God created mankind only to end up sending most people to Hell.

They also erred in assuming that God exclusively used an **absolute** standard of judgement on people—instead of also a **relative** one—depending on circumstances. That is, **God has <u>two</u> ways to judge people—depending on their level of awareness**.

If a person lived in a time and place **where they <u>knew</u> about Jesus—God the Father honors his Son Jesus by having all prayers for salvation go through Him (see the Prayer for Salvation at the end of this book).** This is the absolute standard of judgement. But if people lived in a time or place that had never heard of Jesus, **God does <u>not</u> automatically condemn them all to Hell**—as many people in the past believed (out of ignorance, not ill will).

Instead, **God uses a <u>relative</u> standard of judgement with all people who either never heard of Jesus or never understood his role as the <u>exclusive</u> intermediary between God and mankind for salvation in the afterlife**. Speaking of Jesus, the Bible tells us in *Acts* 4:12,

> **"Salvation is found in no one else, for there is no other name under heaven given to mankind by which we must be saved."**

Jesus himself in *John* 14: 6 says of himself,

> **"I am the way and the truth and the life. No one comes to the Father except through me."**

Still again, Jesus describes his role as the gateway to God and salvation in *John* 10:9,

> **"I am the gate; whoever enters through me will be saved"**

So you can see the problem. **If the <u>only</u> way to God is through Jesus Christ—what happens to the many billions of souls who have never heard of Jesus or—if they have heard of him—never properly understood his exclusive role in the salvation of all people?**

So what God does is this. Since God knows all things—he is able to tell if a person <u>would have accepted</u> Jesus as his Lord and Savior, if he <u>had</u> lived in a time and place where the name and power of Jesus was known. **If God knows that a person would have accepted Jesus, if he had had the chance to—that is sufficient. He will grant that person eternal salvation in Heaven**. To think otherwise—as many people have done in the past—is to 'dumb' God down to our level.

Lesson #2

Is Life Fair?

God saw all that he had made,
and it was very good.
(*Genesis* 1:31)

Yes, because everyone gets what they deserve. Actually, they get even <u>more</u> than they deserve. We also know life is fair because the world was designed and created by an entirely holy and just God who cannot tolerate injustice or evil. **God cannot create something contrary to his nature.** But because people have too many misconceptions about such spiritual matters, we will have to pause and explain what we mean—point by point. Otherwise people will quickly shut down and reject such arguments—however biblically grounded they are. For **the <u>average</u> person's understanding of God and life is <u>exactly the opposite</u> of the way they really are.**

1 John 3:20 tells us that **God knows everything.** This **includes the future.** Before any of us were born—before God even created the world—he looked out into the future. **He foresaw how <u>receptive</u> each person would be** to him and his message. **Based on this information, he designed the world,** all of its history **and** how the **lives of each one of us** would play out in full detail.

We may call **each person's receptivity** to God, their <u>Spiritual Disposition Factor</u>—or <u>SDF</u>. **People** that God foresaw—before the creation of the world—had **high** SDF, would go on to **lead lives**—when they were eventually born—**of high spirituality and** eventual **salvation in Living Heaven. People** with **mid-level SDF** would go on to **lead lives of average spirituality** and would **end up in Dead Heaven.** Those that God foresaw had **low-level SDF** would have low spirituality and **end up in Hell because** of **their evil deeds and rejection of God**.

We see **SDF** illustrated **in the Parable of the Talents** that Jesus tells in *Matthew* 25:14-30. In the story, a master (= Jesus) is about to go on a long journey (= going up to heaven after his crucifixion). He calls three of his servants before he goes. He gives to each of them a certain number of **talents**. The term originally meant **units of money** until it switched to its current meaning of **'ability'** due to the fame of this parable. This is because money gives you the ability to do things with it.

The **number of talents** the master gives to each servant—the text tells us—**is based on the <u>ability</u> of each one**. To one servant he gives 5 talents. To another he gives 2 talents. To the third one, he gives only 1 talent.

The servants are to invest the master's money so that when he returns, the amount of money he has, will have increased because of their efforts. When the master returns, he demands an accounting from each servant as to what they did with his money. This symbolizes Judgement Day before God in heaven that all of us will one day face.

The one who was given 5 talents—earned another 5 talents for their master. The one given 2—earned another 2. The one who was given one talent—hid it and didn't earn any additional money for his master. **The servants who increased their master's money are praised, while the one who earned no increase is cursed**. He is sent to **'outer darkness'** where there is 'weeping and gnashing of teeth' (= **Hell**).

The amount of money (= ability to do spiritual good) each servant is given—reflects their pre-birth SDF. **The <u>potential</u> for spiritual good that people have entering the world <u>always matches</u> the <u>actual</u> spiritual good they manage to do by the end of their life.** The servant with an SDF of 5—earns in his life 5. The one with an SDF of 2—earns 2. Unfortunately, **in the case of the third servant, the proportionality—which <u>does</u> exist in real life—breaks down in our story for logistical reasons.**

The text wants to stress that the servant earned <u>no</u> income for his master—which is what many people today do. **They never win any souls for Christ or do any good deeds for God**. But you couldn't have a story where a servant wasn't given <u>any</u> coins and then is expected to parlay his o coins into more. Nor could you have someone given just ½ a coin—which is implausible—so that he gives a whole coin back. But the point is—**the servant with low SDF—did little or nothing for his master with it**. For that, his master **sent him to Hell** to be punished.

The various **servants,** of course, **represent all of us**. We are all servants of that master—Jesus—and **we are** likewise **required on Judgement Day to give an accounting of our life** in terms of how we used the abilities God gave us. **If you did not increase God's wealth in terms of souls won to heaven or good deeds done—you will be** like the servant given 1 talent who was **sent to Hell. Beware**.

Some eastern religions correctly perceived that we have some impact—before our birth—on the way our life on earth plays out. That 'impact' is our SDF. But eastern religions were wrong to assume we live multiple lives and that it is our <u>prior</u> lives that determine our current one. We only live <u>once</u>.

Our SDF or receptivity to God—is <u>not</u> 'works' since we are not alive yet to <u>do</u> any deeds. God merely detects in us—before we are born—that we are <u>receptive</u> to accepting him—if we were to ever hear the message about him. The reason this matters is that *Ephesians* 2:8-9 warns us:

> "It is by grace [= God's favor undeserved by us] you
> have been saved, through faith—and this is not from
> yourselves, it is the gift of God—not by works, so
> that no one can boast."

God's simple foreknowledge—before we are born—of how receptive we will be towards him—is <u>in no way earning salvation</u> by our own efforts or works.

But can we really have free will to act—if God already knows the future? There is a subtle balance between the actions we <u>can</u> take—and the actions God foreknows we <u>will</u> take. In theory, we can take actions that are contrary to what God foresaw we would do. So **we have free will**. But in actual practice—every time—the actions that seem good to us to take—always happen to be what God foreknew we would do. This is because **God knows us and our inclinations better than we know ourselves**. Knowing us in expert detail, God always puts us in situations where the course of action that seems best to us to take at the time—is what he foreknew we would do.

We <u>always</u> retain the free will to act. But God knows our inclinations and controls the environments he puts us into—thus creating consistently predictable and foreknowable actions on our part. The **Bible freely admits** that **God directs** or guides **our actions** in this way. For example,

"A person's steps are directed by the Lord. How then can anyone understand their own way?" (*Proverbs* 20:24)

AND

"In their hearts people plan their course, but the Lord establishes their steps." (*Proverbs* 16:9)

Notice how—in the two quotes above—the Bible does not say that God directs only <u>believers'</u> steps, but <u>all</u> people's steps—believers or not. Pause for a moment to let this idea sink in. This means that **people who hate God and think they are rebelling against him and all that he stands for—are actually being <u>directed</u>** by him and <u>serving his overall purpose</u> **in world history**.

Judas Iscariot is a good example of this. He was responsible for betraying Jesus to the religious authorities which led to Jesus' death on the cross. **God sent Jesus into the world in order that he might die as a sacrifice before God for the sins' of humanity**. He <u>had</u> to die. Judas—in being the one to betray him—probably thought he was acting on his own will and volition. He was. But he was at the same time fulfilling the very role God wanted him to play. **Everything that happens in the world—now and throughout all of history—does not just happen randomly on its own. Rather, God directs it according to a predetermined 'script' in his mind that he wants to happen.**

HISTORICAL ERROR

Bible scholars in the past had a hard time with the concept of free will vs. predestination. They assumed there could only be free will (= complete freedom for people to choose) or predestination (= complete control by God). The reality—as often—lies in the middle. People have free will to choose their actions—but God does 'nudge' them to choose a certain way. Since people can resist this nudging, it does not constitute predestination by God.

Further evidence of God's direction of events and complete knowledge of human affairs occurs in *Matthew* 10:29-30 where Jesus tells us,

> "Are not two sparrows sold for a penny?
> Yet not one of them will fall
> to the ground outside of your Father's
> will" And even the very hairs of
> your head are all numbered."

So **why does God have to direct all the events of the world? To make sure nothing goes wrong. Every single thing—to the tiniest detail—that happens to you and everyone else in this world—is directed and planned out by God with his full awareness and approval. This is how he guarantees the world is just and fair.** God himself is just and fair and he must ensure that the creatures he brings to live in it—people and animals—are treated justly and fairly.

Without this extensive direction—actual evil or unjust things

<u>could</u> **happen**. Take, for example, someone whose high SDF says they are fated to do many good things in the world. **If—by odd circumstance—they are suddenly killed before they can do them—they would be denied a credit for good that they were entitled to.** In a hypothetical case like this, they would get <u>less</u> than they deserved.

In this and all similar cases, the world <u>would</u> be unfair and unjust. Some people would get less than they deserve, while others would get more than they deserve. To prevent this evil from happening, **God directs the outcome of <u>all</u> events that take place in the world.** This is a <u>good</u> thing since it ensures that everything that happens is fair and just. This is why *Romans* 8:28 tells us,

"All things work together for good to those who love God"

So—if God is good and directs everything that happens so that it always turns out for the good—why do so many people think the world is evil? Because they lack proper spiritual discernment.

There is an **'earthly' understanding** of things and a **'spiritual' understanding** of things. God made them **exact opposites**. **All people** born into this world **automatically possess earthly understanding**. But **only people** who are **'born again'**—who have achieved **salvation** from God—**possess spiritual understanding** which God gives us **in varying degrees based on** our SDF towards him. **People with spiritual understanding <u>can</u> understand the workings of God** in the world—while **those with just earthly understanding <u>can't</u>**.

Indeed, since God designed these two types of understanding to be opposites, **those who possess only the one type— earthly understanding—will view the opposite type—spiritual understanding—as upside down or mere foolishness.** *1 Corinthians* 2:14 addresses this,

"The person without the Spirit does not
accept the things that come from
the Spirit of God but considers them
foolishness, and cannot understand
them because they are discerned only through the Spirit"

People with only earthly understanding—the average person—will perceive the world as full of <u>actual</u> evil. This is the upside down view of things that is the exact <u>opposite</u> of reality. This view slanders God by accusing him of being evil—for creating a world that contains <u>actual</u> evil. **People with true spiritual understanding know that the world only <u>appears</u> to be evil—but in fact is <u>actually</u> good.**

Let us give some examples now to illustrate how this works. The death of a newborn baby—from an earthly understanding—is regarded as a terrible evil. We think of the pain and suffering the child endured and mourn the loss of all its potential in life.

From a spiritual perspective—the baby dying was a <u>good</u> thing. Because the baby lacks a moral awareness of good and evil, it goes straight to God's loving presence in Living Heaven for eternity. It doesn't have to toil away here on earth—in a lesser existence—for a lifetime.

'The Good Die Young'

As far as God and the Bible are concerned—this classic proverb is very <u>true</u>: **all fetuses, babies, young children and all who—by reason of some impairment—lack moral awareness of good and evil—go directly to Living Heaven at death.**

We have seen St. Paul's theological statement of this in *Romans* 4:15,

"Where there is no law [= moral awareness of good and evil] there is no sin"

But we even have God himself verify this with the ancient Israelites and the Promised Land. **The Israelites symbolize every man's spiritual journey.** God chose them to enter the **Promised Land (= a metaphor for Living Heaven).** But most of the <u>adults</u> who wandered in the wilderness for 40 years—who <u>did</u> possess moral awareness—doubted God and grumbled against him. Angry at this, God said,

> "'Not one of the men of this evil generation shall see the good land I swore to give to your fathers,' but '**your children who** on that day **did not know good from evil—will enter the land that I will give them and they will possess it.**'" (*Deuteronomy* 1:35 and 1:39)

People who God assigns the fate of dying young—based on their high or relatively high SDF—<u>are</u> in fact viewed by him as good—as the proverb correctly observes. As we said earlier, if some adversity or 'evil' befalls you <u>undeserved</u>—as is the case with young children—God compensates you with a <u>greater</u> spiritual good. In this case, an eternity of bliss in Living Heaven in God's presence.

From a spiritual perspective, the baby in our story who died—did very well for itself. Less than 17% of all people make it to Living Heaven. Statistically, **most of the people grieving the death of that baby—will themselves <u>not</u> make it to Living Heaven.** That 'poor' baby was far more fortunate than most of them.

The Spiritual Law of Opposites

The baby in our example also helps illustrate the important Spiritual Law of Opposites. We said that **earthly understanding** and

spiritual understanding were opposites in nature. This is because God made the respective worlds they represent—the Material World and the Spiritual World—opposite in nature in spiritual terms.

The Spiritual Law of Opposites is a simple and useful guide for understanding people's spiritual status in life. It states:

Bad in this world = Good in the next world (and vice-versa)

The Law of Opposites **is my paraphrase of Jesus' words** to us in *Matthew* 20:16:

"The last will be first, and the first will be last"

The relationship between the Material World and the Spiritual World is actually more complicated. In **spiritual** terms, these two worlds are opposites. But in **physical** terms, God made them parallel to each other. We will discuss this more later and explain the reason for his doing this.

Let us apply this law to **the baby** in our example who died young. It **had 'bad' in this world, so it will have 'good' in the next world or afterlife**. Jesus died young—having been tortured and crucified on the cross. This too is bad in this world. But, as a result of his sacrificial death for mankind, God glorified and exalted him—a good thing in the eternal next world.

> **"God exalted Him to the highest place and gave Him the name above all names, that at the name of Jesus every knee should bow, in heaven and on earth, and every tongue confess that Jesus Christ is Lord"** (*Philippians* 2:9-10)

So we can see provided that our perspective encompasses <u>both</u> worlds—this one and the next—that **there is no <u>actual</u> evil in our world God created, just <u>apparent</u> evil**. What appears from a human perspective to be 'evil'—like our baby dying young—is actually a good thing because, from a spiritual perspective, the baby thereby earned bliss for eternity.

So it is with <u>everything</u> in our world. **God strictly controls all events that occur down to the <u>tiniest</u> detail.** God knows even the number of hairs on our heads. God also rewards all <u>undeserved</u> adversity with <u>greater</u> good. So, as a result, **we live in a just and fair world created by a just and fair God.**

Those who choose to see (apparent) evil, do so because they are <u>unspiritual</u> and only see life through an earthly perspective. They either <u>can't or refuse</u> to see life from a <u>spiritual</u> perspective that shows us that God generously overcompensates us with greater spiritual good for any undeserved adversity we may experience. Without this essential spiritual perspective—one's view of the world is upside down and the exact <u>opposite</u> of truth.

Let us now apply the Law of Opposites to view other aspects of people's lives. But before we do this—let us briefly mention how animals fit in to all this. **Animals have not been given much in this life**. Most of them live only a brief time, lead lives of great struggle for existence and often die a violent death at the hand of predators or rivals. **The bad they experience in this life is compensated by God with good in the next life—Living Heaven.** This Law is <u>yet another way</u> to show that animals make it to Living Heaven when they die—just like young children.

<u>Unlike</u> those who die young or experience great hardship in life of some sort, **there is no special spiritual reward that God gives us in the next life if we live long, healthy and prosperous lives in <u>this</u> life. The earthly good you experience in this life is <u>all</u> there is**. It is only undeserved <u>evil</u> that God must compensate you for.

According to the Law of Opposites, people who live long, healthy and financially prosperous lives (= **good in this life**)—will have **bad in the next life**. This is **true**. Statistically, as we have seen, most such people will <u>not</u> make it to Living Heaven. Most will be condemned to Dead Heaven—a few to Hell. Why is this?

Most people, if they are **given a comfortable life in this world, will <u>not</u> be motivated to sacrifice and deny themselves in order to please God and advance his Kingdom on earth.** They may do a little—but not very much. They become the **'lukewarm'** type of person that—as we saw—**God says** in *Revelation* 3:16 that **he will spit out of his mouth.**

Jesus—in a famous passage in *Matthew* 19:23-24—tells us about the chances of a rich person faring well on Judgement Day in the afterworld,

> **"'Truly I tell you, it is hard for someone who is rich to enter the kingdom of heaven. Again I tell you, it is easier for a camel to go through the eye of a needle than for someone who is rich to enter the kingdom of God.'"**

THE SYMBOLIC NATURE OF OLD TESTAMENT IMAGERY

Matthew 19:25—the verse just after the above quote—tells us that **Jesus' disciples were 'greatly astonished' to hear Jesus say it is hard for rich people to enter heaven.** This is because they had grown up with a <u>literal</u> view of Old Testament imagery. They had all read that the early Patriarchs—like Abraham—were wealthy in terms of their possessions. So **they concluded that if someone possessed great earthly wealth, it was a sign of God's favor.** But their interpretation was exactly the <u>opposite</u> of the truth—because when interpreting Old Testament imagery, we must realize:

What is <u>literal and physical</u> in the Old Testament— should be interpreted as <u>figurative and spiritual</u> (just as New Testament imagery is figurative and spiritual)

The **early Patriarchs' literal, physical wealth symbolized that they were <u>spiritually</u> wealthy because of their close relationship with God**. Logically, this <u>must</u> be the case. We just saw—in Jesus' words—how hard it is for a rich person to enter heaven. **<u>Earthly</u> wealth (= money) creates a barrier between a person and God.**

Reading Old Testament Literal Language <u>Spiritually</u> is Essential

Being aware that you must frequently substitute the Old Testament's literal meaning for a spiritual one—is <u>key</u> to properly understanding the Bible. *Malachi* 4:5—the next to last verse in the Old Testament—has God tell us,

> "See, I will send the prophet Elijah to you before that great and
> dreadful day of the Lord comes."

Because of this verse, people in Jesus' day were expecting the <u>literal</u> prophet Elijah to precede the Messiah. But *Luke* 1:17 tells us of John the Baptist,

> **"He will go on before the Lord, in the spirit and power of Elijah"**

Because converting <u>literal to spiritual</u> is so important when reading the Old Testament, Jesus made it a point to train his disciples to do this—so they could better understand scripture. For example, at one point in *Matthew* 16, Jesus tells his disciples to 'beware the yeast of the Pharisees.' This gets them caught up in a discussion among themselves about literal bread. *Matthew* 16:11-12 tells us that Jesus then responds,

> "'How is it you don't understand that I
> was not talking to you about

bread? But be on your guard against the
yeast of the Pharisees and
Sadducees.' Then they understood that he was not telling them to
guard against the yeast used in bread,
but against the teaching of the
Pharisees and Sadducees."

We see the toxicity of earthly wealth to your soul in the story of Jesus and the Rich Young Man in *Matthew* 19:16-22. There a rich young man turns away from following Jesus because he didn't want to give up—as Jesus had told him to—his great earthly wealth to obtain treasure in heaven. And so it is with most people who have earthly riches. **But true <u>spiritual</u> wealth does not push you away from God. Rather, it reflects how spiritually close you are to God.**

God Actively <u>Blocks</u> the Spiritually 'Unworthy' From Understanding His Word

Be aware that—in the New Testament—information is presented to you <u>directly</u>. You don't have the Old Testament 'veil'—as St. Paul calls it in *2 Corinthians* 3:15—to block or inhibit your understanding. This **veil** is the reality that the **Law in the Old Testament is encoded by God 'upside down'. That is, you must always convert the imagery presented to you from literal to figurative in order to properly understand it (= make it right side up).**

If you do not do this, your understanding of things will be upside down—the exact opposite of the truth. This was the case—as we saw—with Jesus' disciples who were shocked to hear that <u>literal</u> earthly wealth didn't ensure you an easy entrance into heaven. Only <u>spiritual</u> wealth with God does this.

Paul says in *2 Corinthians* 3:14 that this veil hindered the spiritual understanding of his fellow Jews when reading scripture,

> "But their minds were made dull, for to this day
> the same veil remains when the old covenant [=
> testament] is read. It has not been removed, because
> only in Christ is it taken away."

Because his fellow Jews <u>continued</u> to reject Jesus, Paul adds in the next verse— *2 Corinthians* 3:15—that their spiritual understanding was <u>still</u> being compromised,

> "Even to this day when Moses is read, a veil covers their hearts."

Like putting locks on doors, this coding—inserted by God into scripture—helps keep out or block the spiritually unworthy from heaven.

Jesus' **speaking in parables (= spiritual codes) was another mechanism to keep the spiritually unworthy from understanding.** When his disciples ask him why he does this, Jesus responds in *Mark* 4:11-12,

> "The secret of the kingdom of God has been given to you. But
> to those on the outside everything is said in parables so that,
> 'they may be ever seeing but never perceiving, and ever hearing
> but never understanding; otherwise they
> might turn and be forgiven"

Yet **another way for God to deceive the spiritually unworthy** is to trick them with what I call '**Biblical booby traps**'. These are **things that God deliberately puts into the Bible that he knows will spiritually trip up people who are hostile to God and unworthy of understanding and salvation**. These include depictions of God in human form walking around the Garden of Eden or people living to almost 1000 years of age in the book of *Genesis*. We will deal with these in some depth later in the book.

But the **biggest way that God keeps the spiritually unworthy from understanding** is—as we said—by **making spiritual wisdom** and earthly wisdom exact <u>opposites</u>. Spiritual wisdom is so far apart from earthly understanding that it appears—to the non-spiritual person—to be 'foolishness'. **Unless God himself comes to you to help you understand it—you will <u>never</u> understand it.**

Veils, parables, booby traps and making wisdom counterintuitive—are all devices God uses to 'lock out' the unworthy from heaven. And they are all necessary. If an unrepentant evil man somehow knew the right words to say and prayers to make—God would <u>have</u> to forgive him and grant him salvation ('otherwise they [= the evil doers] might turn and be forgiven'). That is why God uses them.

Just as spiritual wisdom is foolishness—to someone with only earthly understanding— Paul says in *1 Corinthians* 3:19 that the opposite is true as well,

"The wisdom of this world is foolishness in God's sight."

Then, quoting *Job* 5:13 from the Old Testament, Paul adds,

"As it is written: 'He catches the wise in their craftiness'"

That is, **for those who try to use tricks against God to sneak into heaven undeservedly, he has his aforementioned blocking devices in place to keep all such people out of heaven.** It really is a futile task to try to trick God. Before you were ever born—even before the creation of the universe—God knew in advance <u>every</u> <u>trick</u> you would one day try to pull against him in your life.

Let us return now to the topic of wealth. In the New Testament, you will observe that **nobody prominent in the early church was wealthy in earthly terms.** Not Jesus—nor any of his apostles nor Paul. In fact, in the early church—as soon as a person converted— **they would give away all their wealth** to the poor and to sustain the church as a whole. *Acts* 2:44-45 says,

"All the believers were together and had
everything in common. They sold
property and possessions to give to anyone who had need."

Compare this lifestyle with today's televangelists and other ministers who lead extravagantly self-indulgent and wealthy lives at the expense of their church members—and the true Gospel. What will the likely fate of such people be on Judgement Day?

Since God has set up all these blocking devices to hinder the understanding of the spiritually unworthy—and therefore their ability to achieve salvation—<u>you must come to Jesus</u> for help</u>. Otherwise you will see things <u>upside down</u>—exactly the opposite of the way they really are. **Jesus must come and remove the 'veil' from you so you can see clearly**.

This **whole system God has set up** is all **very deliberate**. Nobody gets into heaven by accident or sheer luck. **<u>You can only enter heaven by honoring Jesus</u>**—who God the Father exalted to this position of **exclusive gatekeeper to God and heaven. See the <u>Prayer for</u> <u>Salvation</u> at the end of this book to start your entrance into heaven right now.**

People who are wealthy and powerful in this life are too attached to this world and care too little for God and his kingdom. This is especially true if these people became wealthy and powerful by doing jobs that **actively advance the Satanic agenda in the world**. Such people—along with all <u>explicit</u> practitioners of evil like witchcraft, sorcery and the occult—are headed, not for just Dead Heaven—but Hell itself.

To avoid going to Hell—or even Dead Heaven—you must do the following. Since Jesus won salvation for people at the sacrifice of his own life—God exalted him to the highest levels. He made Jesus the exclusive gateway to God and salvation for people. *Acts 4:12* tells us,

"Salvation is found in no one else, for there is no other name under heaven given to mankind by which we must be saved."

St. Paul in *Romans* 10:9-10 adds,

> **"If you declare with your mouth, "Jesus is Lord," and believe in your heart that God raised him from the dead, you will be saved. For it is with your heart that you believe and are justified, and it is with your mouth that you profess your faith and are saved."**

Jesus is the only gateway to God (the Father), forgiveness and Living Heaven. Jesus himself says this in *John* 14:6,

> **"I am the way and the truth and the life. No one comes to the Father except through me."**

So Jesus is the only one judging all petitions from people to God for salvation and entrance to Living Heaven. As we saw, he uses two different standards of judgment: an **absolute** one and a **relative** one—based on one's degree of knowledge or understanding.

He uses the absolute standard of judgement with adults who possess moral awareness of good and evil and who don't have any intellectual or mental health impairments. This would include—most likely—all those reading this book. These people must—while still alive—profess to Jesus their faith in him, renounce their prior sins and resolve to follow God to the best of their ability.

Jesus uses a simpler <u>relative</u> standard of judgement with everyone else—those who are not able to make a direct appeal to him as those in absolute judgement do. These—as we have seen—include all animals and lower life forms, all human beings who lack moral awareness and all who are not of sound mind.

It also includes all people who lived in a time or place that never knew about Jesus.

To summarize, all those who have a legitimate reason why they can't do the absolute judgement before Jesus—will be judged by him according to the relative system. <u>But he will judge every creature appearing before him in one of these two ways</u>.

Two Types of Spirituality: Active and Passive

There are two types of 'good' spirituality that bring our soul closer to God and enhance our position in the afterlife: **Active Spirituality (AS)** and **Passive Spirituality (PS). Active spirituality is all the good deeds you do—like feeding the poor, praying for those in need and giving to those less fortunate**. Passive Spirituality is <u>undeserved</u> adversity or 'apparent evil' that befalls you. As we saw earlier—**this could be dying young, suffering debilitating health conditions or any kind of adversity or hardship that afflicts you**.

People of high spirituality will obviously have a lot of Active Spirituality in their spiritual resume. But **because the <u>genuine</u> church will always be persecuted by the Satanic earthly forces opposed to its spread—real believers will also experience a lot of Passive Spirituality**. So Jesus did great deeds on earth (AS) and then died on the cross and spent 3 days in Hell to reconcile mankind to God (AS and PS at the same time). 11 out of the 12 apostles of Jesus died violent deaths (PS) after lifetimes spent witnessing to the Gospel of Jesus and converting people (AS). St. Paul after a lifetime of founding and supporting churches all over the Mediterranean area (AS) recounts for us in *2 Corinthians* 11:24-28 some of the hardships (PS) he also had to undergo along the way,

> "Five times I received from the Jews the forty lashes minus one. Three times I was beaten with rods, once I was pelted with stones, three times I was shipwrecked, I spent a night and a day in the open sea, I have been constantly on the move.

I have been in danger from rivers, in danger from bandits, in danger from my fellow Jews, in danger from Gentiles, in danger in the city, in danger in the country, in danger at sea; and in danger from false believers. I have labored and toiled and have often gone without sleep; I have known hunger and thirst and have often gone without food; I have been cold and naked. Besides everything else, I face daily the pressure of my concern for all the churches."

After all this, Paul was later imprisoned in Rome and then crucified, earning him additional PS.

The *Book of Acts* in the New Testament shows us what a genuinely spiritual, flourishing church looks like. There is a lot of Active Spirituality to be found because all church members feel obliged to act. In the satanically infiltrated churches of today, the situation is very different. There is very little AS among the rank and file members. They have been satanically conditioned to be passive. Basically, just show up once a week and you have done your duty. Some don't even bother to show up every week.

If you are confronted with evil every once in a while—or need to minister to someone, just let the minister take care of everything. The rank and file don't in general feel the need to be doing this sort of thing themselves.

Our current state of affairs didn't just happen. **The Satanists—acting both outside and inside the church—designed it this way. They have encouraged the modern church to not be like the vigorous ancient church seen in the Book of Acts**. Satanists for the most part don't act openly—but are like actors when they infiltrate the church and society. **They play the role of pious clergyman, respectable businessman, politician, journalist or entertainer, etc.**

But **they introduce agendas into their various fields—** designed by higher-ups in the Satanic world and ordered by them to be implemented on a timetable—that have cumulatively changed our society (and the whole world) for the worse over time.

They have corrupted churches and schools with their teachings, harmed our economy, flooded the airwaves with moral filth, got us into continuous wars and conflicts and deceived the public. They give them false explanations for everything that don't allow people to see who and what is <u>really</u> behind current events and the changes in our society.

It is every believer's duty to actively resist such evil— whenever it arises. And so—given the massive Satanic forces arrayed against believers and the whole world—we may lay down the following rule:

Passivity in the face of evil—is evil.

By not actively fighting evil—**God implicates <u>you</u> in that evil. Not fighting evil when you are able to—is effectively <u>condoning</u> it**. But not even the quote above is complete. We must revise it further:

Passivity is evil.

We have only a very <u>limited</u> time to act—both as individuals and collectively as the global church. **Soon the drama of human history will come to a close and there will be no more time to act. We will all then face immediate judgement before God. We all must do all we can with the very limited time we have left. We cannot squander it.**

One Reason 'Bad' Things Happen to Good People is Because God Loves Them

In periods of low spirituality—like today—people have low levels of Active Spirituality. They are not doing a lot of active spiritual good deeds. **If people do not achieve enough good by** <u>**doing**</u> **good in the form of Active Spirituality, then the only way for them to achieve greater amounts of good is to suffer hardship (undeserved) sent to them by God that will grant them good through Passive Spirituality.** That means they will experience more debilitating—even fatal—health conditions, more financial or relationship problems or general stressful incidents in their lives.

This especially happens with people who can be described by the following saying,

"The spirit is willing, but the flesh is weak"

God observes that **this type of people** tend to **have relatively high SDF** because their 'spirit <u>is</u> willing' to follow God. The problem is **they are too lazy** in actual practice to carry out all that their spirit would like—in theory—to do for God.

When there exists a large disparity between a person's low level of <u>achieved</u> **spiritual good and a high level of SDF** <u>predicted</u> **good, God will step in to help. He will boost their level of achieved good—by boosting their** <u>Passive</u> **Spirituality levels by sending them great adversity to overcome.**

By doing this, **people's total levels of achieved good—Active and Passive—get boosted so that they now** <u>match</u> **their high potential for good (= receptivity or SDF).** There is now exact proportionality between people's predicted potential for good and their actual accomplished good.

This is equivalent to the story of the Parable of the Talents. The servants who started out with 5 or 10 talents (= their potential for good) were both able to earn this exact amount (= actual accomplishment of good) to give back to their master and enrich him.

Now the hardship God sends to people to boost their Passive Spirituality—when their Active Spirituality levels are too low—can come in many forms: from cancer, to a car crash, to a job loss, divorce, etc.

This large boost of good can work wonders in a person's

spiritual life. If someone isn't saved yet—it may prompt them to become saved. Or if they are saved, the good from the Passive Spirituality they endured, may spur them on to do good deeds to boost their Active Spirituality as well. And with this boost of good from adversity—which the world would call 'evil'—many people who would otherwise end up in Dead Heaven—or even Hell—will actually make it to Living Heaven. So is it 'evil' of God to let someone get cancer if they—in so doing—go from Hell to Living Heaven?

This and everything else that God does is out of love for people. If they are good-natured people, but not doing enough good deeds through Active Spirituality, he will help them out with a boost of good from the adversity of Passive Spirituality.

That is why it often seems that it is the nice person at the office you work at who gets the terrible diagnosis of cancer—not the insufferable jerk. That is probably because God isn't helping the jerk at the office. The jerk, very likely, is hostile to God with low SDF and low overall levels of good. He likely—in addition—is rejecting all of God's overtures to him. You can only help the willing.

St. Paul in the Bible was initially hostile to Christ and Christianity—because of his zeal for what he thought was Judaism was misplaced. Once corrected, he happily accepted God. Not all the strongly resistant to God are like Paul, however. Some people never learn—except maybe when they are in Hell.

Lesson #3

Why Doesn't God Just Reveal Himself So Everyone Will Believe in Him?

Because that would <u>ruin</u> everything. The moment people didn't just suspect—but knew with <u>100% certainty</u> that God existed—our relationship toward God would change drastically. It would go from **'state of faith'** to **'state of knowledge'**. As a result, everyone alive today—that wasn't already saved—would immediately be condemned to Hell for eternity. It is the most calamitous scenario possible for mankind—worse even than a nuclear war which would kill the physical body, but not affect the afterlife of one's soul.

If we knew <u>for certain</u> that God existed—then faith would no longer exist. You can only have faith with things that you have some <u>doubt</u> about. **Certain knowledge eliminates faith**. Here is the problem. The Bible in *Hebrews* 11:6 tells us,

"Without faith it is impossible to please God."

Why is this? Because our righteousness—in God's eyes—is pathetically low. *Isaiah* 64:6 says,

"All our righteous acts are like filthy rags"

Psalms 14:3 adds,

"There is no one who does good, not even one"

Romans 3:23 confirms,

"All have sinned and fall short of the glory of God"

Because mankind is so hopelessly sinful—there is no way we can please God with any of our spiritual good deeds. **All we can offer is our faith in God**. We don't know for certain that God exists. But we still take a leap of faith and trust God when he says he exists. **This pleases him—and is the only thing we can do that pleases him. But we need to be in a 'state of faith' toward God for this to happen**.

If we know for certain that God exists—God would be forced to switch how he judges us. Why? Because God always follows his EOF law of proportionality with us. More on this later in the chapter. **The more knowledge of him we possess—the more accountable we are before him**. As a result, we would go from a 'relative' standard of judgement to an 'absolute' one. Under the milder relative standard of judgement, God only charges you with sin if you knew beforehand that an act you committed was wrong. **You guilt is relative or proportional to your level of knowledge of right and wrong**. Sins that you unknowingly commit or that you accidentally or unintentionally commit—don't therefore count as sins under relative justice. Also, under relative justice, you have a chance to find forgiveness for your sins.

But **under absolute justice**—things are much harsher. Nobody cares what your state of knowledge was when you committed a sin. **A sin is a sin whether you committed it knowingly, unknowingly or accidentally**. That is, sin in an absolute system isn't dependent on moral awareness or anything else. It stands as a sin in absolute, unqualified terms. Even worse, once you have committed a sin under an absolute standard of justice—that sin will never be forgiven. You are guaranteed to go to hell forever because of it.

If God applied this brutally harsh standard of **absolute justice on us, everyone—except the currently saved—would be condemned to hell for eternity**. **We need faith to exist so we can stay under the current, milder standard of relative judgement**.

<u>**So that is why God doesn't openly reveal himself to us**</u>—to answer the question that opened this chapter.

But Doesn't It Say in the Bible that People <u>Saw</u> God?

Isn't this proof of his existence? Didn't God speak to Moses in the form of a burning bush? Didn't God appear to the nation of Israel as a pillar of cloud by day and a pillar of fire by night during the 40 years they wandered in the Sinai Desert? Doesn't it say that Moses spoke face to face with God at the Tent of Meeting and on Mount Sinai?

The *Gospel of John* 1:18 says, **"no one has ever seen God."** The **burning bush, cloud and fire imagery** in the Old Testament were **representations of God—but not God himself. Descriptions of God speaking to Moses 'face to face' are simply a metaphor** indicating the close relationship in spirit the two had. **God, the Bible tells us, is a spirit** (*John* 4:24) **that fills all of heaven and earth** (*Jeremiah* 23:24). Likewise, in *Matthew* 5:8 in the Sermon on the Mount when Jesus tells us,

> **"Blessed are the pure in heart,**
> **for they will see God."**

This means the pure in heart will have a close communion with God in their spirit—and <u>one day</u> will see him in Living Heaven in the afterlife. **So we currently remain in a <u>state of faith</u> toward God— so it is <u>still</u> possible for people to be saved—precisely because no one has literally seen him.**

Isn't Jesus supposed to be God? Didn't many people see him during his time on earth? Now while it is true that **Jesus is one of the 3 persons of God—along with God the Father and the Holy Spirit**—that **does <u>not</u> change things** here. **Jesus** incarnated or **appeared to people on earth as a <u>man</u>** and called himself the Son of Man. **People did not know <u>for a fact</u> that he was God**—even when his spirit ascended to heaven. Others, such as the prophet Elijah, were also taken up to heaven at the end of their lives.

So **forgiveness is possible for those who did not recognize him as God.**

But—notoriously—**this is <u>not</u> the case with the Holy Spirit**. When the Holy Spirit acts in this world, he does not 'disguise' himself as a person—like Jesus did, being born of a father and mother. This provided people with plausible deniability not to believe that Jesus is God. Indeed, the Jews to this day do not believe Jesus is God.

But the Holy Spirit is different. The Holy Spirit manifested in our material world to work great miracles at the hands of Jesus. When Jesus was casting out demons by the power of the Holy Spirit, some people accused him of casting out the demons—by the power of <u>**Satan**</u>. Those people who blasphemed the Holy Spirit in this way, got stuck with an example of absolute judgement. **They blasphemed a person of God—the Holy Spirit—working miracles in their midst.**

They couldn't directly see—or necessarily know—that it was the Holy Spirit. But it didn't matter. Since they committed a sin against the Holy Spirit / God—while <u>in the presence of</u> the Holy Spirit / God—they committed the so-called <u>Unpardonable Sin</u>. That is, **a sin committed in the <u>presence</u> of God that condemns them to Hell with no chance of forgiveness ever.**

The Holy Spirit was <u>not</u> disguising himself as a man like Jesus. Rather, he was God acting in the capacity of God on earth. That is why sins against Jesus are treated differently than the sin against the Holy Spirit. **The unpardonable sin is also what God charged the Devil and all the fallen angels with when they rebelled against God—in God's presence.**

Under absolute judgement, it doesn't matter if you <u>knowingly</u> committed a sin or not. <u>Any</u> sin committed for <u>any reason</u> is enough to send you to Hell forever. Because God—in the form of the Holy Spirit—showed up that day in their neighborhood, those blasphemers were then switched—without their knowledge—from relative judgement to absolute judgement.

Jesus says of these people in *Mark* 3:28-30,

> "'Truly I tell you, people can be forgiven all their sins and every slander they utter, but whoever blasphemes against the Holy Spirit will never be forgiven; they are guilty of an eternal sin.' He said this because they were saying, 'He has an impure spirit.'"

Normally, a person only reaches the direct presence of God—and a 'state of knowledge' toward him—<u>when they die</u>. If a person is unsaved when this happens—they automatically go to Hell with no chance for forgiveness. **In the case of the people who blasphemed the Holy Spirit, they didn't have to die and go to the spiritual world. The spiritual world came to them—in the form of the Holy Spirit. But the result is the same**. Unless we are saved, <u>**all of us one day will face this same harsh absolute justice before God on Judgement Day**</u>. <u>**Beware**</u>.

Two great realms exist—the Spiritual world and the Material world—with separate laws for each. God and all spirit beings inhabit the spiritual world. This includes angels, demons and the Devil himself. God's harsh law of absolute justice governs this world. A single sin—as we have seen—will get you banished forever from **God's presence in the spiritual world (= Heaven) to the 'absence' of God's presence (= Hell)—which is also in the spiritual world.**

Hell—By the Way—<u>Isn't</u> Beneath the Earth
Hell—being a spiritual realm—is part of the Spiritual World. It is not located under the earth in our Material World. God exists in one part of the Spiritual World—and the Devil in another. Yet the

Bible also says that God is everywhere. **Heaven is the presence of God, while Hell is the 'absence of God's presence'.** But it is best not to ponder this too deeply. Our Material World—with its space and time—is very differently configured than the Spiritual World which lacks these limiting dimensions.

Under absolute justice, it does not matter how big the sin was or why you committed it. Accidents are not excused nor does anyone care about the circumstances that led up to the sin or that you were unaware it was a sin. Sin here <u>once</u> and you are in hell forever—end of story. The reason justice is so harsh in the spiritual world is basically twofold:

1. **Spirit beings have the equivalent of <u>full adult awareness</u> and capacity to act.** That is, there are no 'baby' angels or demons—equivalent to human babies or young children—who lack full awareness of the consequences of their actions.

2. **Every spirit being either lives now in God's presence in heaven or once did—as in the case of the Devil and his demons. Therefore they stand in a 'state of knowledge' toward God**

This harshness is in keeping with a **spiritual law of proportionality** I will call the **Law of Equal and Opposite Force (EOF)—the spiritual parallel to Newton's 3rd Law of Motion in physics**. God uses this spiritual law when judging his created beings—whether people, animals, angels or demons.

The Bible describes it in *Luke* 12:48 as **"from everyone who has been given much, much will be demanded"**. Its equally true reverse logical corollary would be 'from everyone who has been given little, little will be demanded". **The more awareness of right and wrong you possess when you commit an act, the more**

accountable you are in God's eyes for any sins you commit—and vice-versa.

Jesus addresses this issue in *John* 9:41. There a group of Pharisees rejected some of his words. They then scoff at the notion that they are spiritually blind. Jesus then tells them,

> **"If you were blind [= lacking spiritual awareness], you would not be guilty of sin; but now that you claim you can see, your guilt remains."**

In other words, **as long as the Pharisees were not <u>aware</u> their words were sinful,**

> **God would not charge them with sin**. But then they insist they <u>know</u> exactly what they are saying— and its implications. They <u>then</u> become guilty in God's sight and will be punished accordingly. **One's knowledge or awareness is key**.

A good illustration of this spiritual principle is the way parents treat their own children. If an infant soils its pants—its parents do not fault it. They realize it does not yet know any better and cannot fully control its bodily functions. But what if that same child were to soil his pants as a (healthy) 25 year old adult? Then the parents—and society in general—would fault him for this. What's the difference? The infant was not aware it did anything wrong. But the adult is expected to know better and act accordingly.

God—as the spiritual parent of us all—treats us in the same way that we treat our children. And he plants spiritual teachings—like the example of the infant—in the midst of our daily lives, hoping we will take note. As a result, we can find great profoundness in the simple and ordinary things of life— and in contemplating nature.

The Gospel According to Nature

God—as we have seen—**does not <u>directly</u> reveal himself to mankind**—for the reasons given earlier that include the Unpardonable Sin. But **he does give us <u>indirect</u> clues that he exists and that serve as spiritual guidance for us**. For **he has embedded so many spiritual teachings into nature and our daily lives so that revealed religious texts like the Bible sometimes seem redundant and unnecessary.**

If we carefully observe the world around us—we will quickly realize **we are surrounded by <u>spiritual teachings</u>**. *Psalm* 19:1-4 reveals,

> "The heavens declare the glory of God, the skies proclaim the work of his hands. Day after day they pour forth speech; night after night they display knowledge. There is no speech or language where their voice is not heard. Their voice goes out into all the earth, their words to the ends of the world."

Ominously, Paul in *Romans* 1:20 says that **because God has placed so many spiritual teachings in nature, no one on Judgement Day can claim they did not know about God and matters of right and wrong,**

> "Since the creation of the world God's
> invisible qualities—his eternal
> power and divine nature—have been
> clearly seen, being understood
> from what has been made, **so that men are without excuse.**"

Spiritual World vs. Material World

We saw earlier how God made **spiritual wisdom** and **earthly wisdom** exact opposites. He did this **to** <u>limit</u> **people's understanding** of spiritual wisdom **so that only the spiritually worthy**—those 'to whom the kingdom of God was given'—**would understand** because of God's guidance to them. The exact <u>opposite</u> is the case with the Material World in <u>physical</u> terms. **God designed the physical laws that govern the Material World to <u>parallel</u> spiritual laws that govern the Spiritual World**. By making physical and spiritual laws parallel—that is, the same—God makes it <u>easy</u> for people to understand and draw parallels between the two types of laws—and thereby gain spiritual understanding.

Why would God make it difficult for people in one instance to understand things—and then easy in another instance? **He wants to limit spiritual wisdom to only those who are worthy—that is, those who have <u>high</u> SDF**. So he makes that hard to access. But since God is going to hold everyone on Judgement Day accountable for knowing about him—he places clues all throughout nature as to his existence and power—so everyone will see. All they have to do is look around to see the clues—in nature and our daily lives.

Spiritual teachings—whether found in the Bible or embedded in nature—can be understood on multiple levels. Apparently simple Bible stories—such as that of the serpent tempting Eve in the Garden of Eden—can illustrate a spiritual principle on levels that range from an almost childlike simplicity to extreme complexity.

In the early part of the Bible, God frequently 'dumbs down' spiritual teachings by conveying them through the vehicle of simple stories to accommodate the very simple level of understanding of earlier ages of mankind. Also, **in any given time period, people have varying levels of spiritual sophistication**. Remember that **God gives us only <u>one</u> Bible—but has to make its teachings**

understandable to people from all different times, cultures and levels of spiritual insight.

Rather than give us many different Bibles, God gives us a single Bible that can be read at many levels—from simple to advanced—depending on the sophistication of each age, culture and individual reader. Paul in the New Testament frequently goes back to Old Testament stories to ferret out complex spiritual principles—often by allegorical interpretation—from apparently simple narrative stories about ancient Israel.

In general, the earliest stories of the Bible—especially those in *Genesis*—are the most 'simple'. Later books such as *Romans* and *Hebrews* in the New Testament exhibit far greater complexity. More correctly, the earliest stories of the Bible can be read at multiple levels from simple to advanced—while difficult theology passages from the New Testament are read only at an advanced level.

Mankind by this time—thanks in great degree to St. Paul—had grown up spiritually and was now consuming 'solid food' for adults—no longer needing the spiritual 'milk' appropriate for spiritual infants immature in the faith (see *1 Corinthians* 3:2).

Let us return now to our discussion of spiritual teachings in nature. **I would venture to say that God has probably embedded every single spiritual principle found in the Bible somewhere in nature or in our daily lives.** Some spiritual teachings were gleaned early on by people in many cultures. This is because they are tapping into the same spiritual teachings that God inserted into nature—that we all share. This is why you will find similar teachings in a number of different religions.

As we saw, the spiritual law I call **EOF or Equal and Opposite Force** is an example of a spiritual teaching that is embedded in nature. Its physical parallel in the Material World is **Newton's 3rd Law of Motion in physics**. This states that **for every force there exists an equal and opposite force**. Like the recoil of a gun after a bullet is fired. The force of the bullet going out of the barrel generates an equal force hurling the gun backwards. Spiritually, we see EOF in such verses as *Malachi* 3:7,

> "'**Return to me, and I will return to
> you**,' says the Lord Almighty."

In the Law in the Old Testament, we speak of **'eye for an eye'
retribution**. *Galatians* 6:7 adds,

> **"A man reaps what he sows"**

Jesus says in *Matthew* 7:1-2,

> **"Do not judge or you too will be judged.
> For in the same way you
> judge others, you will be judged, and with the same measure
> you use, it will be measured to you."**

In eastern religions, EOF is better known as 'karma'. In karma,
your actions in a prior life—good or bad—proportionately impact
your current life for good or bad. So, for example, any good you
enjoy in this life is due to the good that you did in a prior life. Any
bad you experience now is due to the bad you did in a past life.

When people get angry at God—without really even
understanding why he allows things to happen as they do—they
are attacking God unjustly and judging him. By cosmic spiritual
decree—EOF—any hatred we direct outward toward others—
including God—only comes back to hurt us.

Because of the EOF Spiritual Law, We <u>Must</u> Forgive

The EOF spiritual law of reciprocity works like a <u>boomerang</u>.
The evil we direct outward to others—in terms of inappropriate
thoughts and deeds—comes back to 'hit' or <u>weaken us</u>. <u>Our
prayers with God carry less weight</u>, and <u>our spiritual status
in heaven is diminished</u>. So—knowing this—**never direct evil
outward**. And **when you are on the <u>receiving end</u> of evil** from
other people's evil thoughts and deeds—**apply forgiveness**. <u>Doing

<u>this converts the</u> <u>incoming evil into good</u>. **You absorb the good—which strengthens you. <u>Your prayers with God carry more weight and your status in heaven is elevated.</u>**

Not thinking evil of others and forgiving others—is not just a 'nice' thing to do, it is an **essential spiritual survival strategy** given God's all-pervasive 'flying' boomerang law of EOF.

Physically, pent-up anger we harbor toward others—and a lack of forgiveness—only ends up hurting our own health. We become stressed, get depressed and alienate others. This includes our loved ones—which only makes us feel worse.

Even in non-religious matters, **God has designed the world to reward—through EOF—people who have faith and to punish people who do not**. If an athlete believes he can make a certain play—he likely will. If he does not believe in his heart he can—he likely will not. In medicine, we have the placebo effect. If a person feels he will get better with a certain medicine, his confidence alone will boost his immune system. Similarly, a hypochondriac who feels he will fall sick because those around him have—likely will. One not so pessimistic—likely will not.

The old proverb 'fortune favors the brave' fits in here. Just substitute God for fortune, and understand that 'the brave' here means people who are confident and have faith. **God has designed the world and its workings to teach us spiritual truths. Positive thinking—and its opposite—work because they mimic or mirror the underlying spiritual reality of EOF.**

Because the universe is the way it is, we must be smart. We must take advantage of the system, instead of being hurt by it. Let us take the example of a basketball player in a simple pick-up game. God punishes the player with missing a clutch shot simply because the player doubted he could make the shot. If this happens in an unimportant basketball game, you can be sure God will punish people in spiritual matters who lack faith or direct anger toward him by the law of EOF.

This does not mean that we will never have any questions about God and his workings. **We will <u>always</u> have questions about God. We live in a world that is 'state of faith'—not full knowledge.** So **by definition we have <u>limited</u> understanding.** Paul addresses this issue of the limited understanding we have in this life—as compared to heaven—in *1 Corinthians* 13:12,

"Now we see but a poor reflection as in a mirror, then we shall see face to face. **Now I know in part, then I shall know fully.**"

One sign that we are approaching the end of the world—will be the <u>noticeable increase</u> in spiritual knowledge and awareness over prior ages and generations. Jesus tells us in *Luke* 12:2,

"There is nothing concealed that will not be revealed, or hidden that will not be made known."

All things hidden spiritually will be revealed. This will culminate **in the Second Coming of Jesus** when **mankind <u>collectively</u> switches from <u>state of faith</u> to <u>state of knowledge</u>. In the past,** this would **only** happen **on an individual basis.** Each person at death would cross over from state of faith to state of knowledge when they entered God's presence in the Spiritual World.

Given the reality of God's EOF spiritual law of reciprocity—it is <u>essential</u> to approach God in the right way. The way you approach him—determines how he will deal with you—as *Psalm* 18:25-26 illustrates (referring to God),

"To the faithful you show yourself faithful, to the blameless you show yourself blameless, to the pure you show yourself pure, but to the crooked you show yourself shrewd"

As you can see, God in all his interactions with us, always follows his EOF spiritual law. But—as the last point indicates—**if we are** deceitful or otherwise immoral, God will never stoop to our level in terms of reciprocity and proportionality. **He always holds on to his holiness and propriety**.

Some foolish people think they can deceive God by living a sinful and self-indulgent life—and then cynically on their deathbed trying to convert. They hope, in so doing, to get the best of both worlds: indulgence in this life and paradise in the next—without any sacrifice or limitations on their behavior.

I can assure you that if this ploy doesn't fool any of us—it does <u>not</u> fool God. In fact, it is probably with this type of person in mind that *Galatians* 6:7-9 warns,

> **"Do not be deceived: God cannot be mocked. A man reaps what he sows. The one who sows to please his sinful nature, from that nature will reap destruction; the one who sows to please the Spirit, from the Spirit will reap eternal life."**

'Reaping destruction' will not be the heaven they hope to achieve. But how foolish is this—given all the Bible says about God judging people on how much spiritual knowledge they have—that people think they can <u>knowingly</u> ignore God for their whole life and then try to trick him at the very end? Their whole life is filled with deceit and contempt for God's intelligence.

With God you cannot have any hypocrisy or discrepancies between what you know to be right and your actions—or your relationship with God will suffer. In *Matthew* 5:20 Jesus shocked his audience when he effectively said that **the <u>entire</u> religious establishment of his day in Israel**—the people you assume are the most holy—**was <u>not</u> going to heaven,**

> **"I tell you that unless your righteousness surpasses that of the Pharisees and the teachers of the law, you will certainly not enter the kingdom of heaven."**

Hypocrisy and lack of effort choked off the spiritual relationship of the religious leaders of ancient Israel **with God. If we are not careful, it will do the** <u>very same thing</u> **to each of us today.** There is a reason Jesus says in *Matthew* 7:13,

"Wide is the path leading to destruction and many follow it"

The reward of **Living Heaven is available to** <u>all</u> of us—but less than 17% of people will actually manage to get there. To do so, **we must all take spirituality and our relationship with God seriously.** In fact, **it must be the** <u>most</u> **important thing in our life. If we put** <u>anything</u> **before God, this is** <u>idolatry</u>—every bit as much as ancient people worshipping statues of pagan gods.

The <u>**first**</u> of the Ten Commandments says in *Exodus* 20:3,

"You shall have no other gods before me."

Many of us today are doing just that. If not a Golden Calf—like the ancient Israelites—we are figuratively worshipping money, power, work, sex, sports, hobbies, etc.

Jesus says **we need to 'take up our cross every day'** (*Luke* 9:23). We need to take **spirituality as seriously as a soldier who fights a war** (2 *Timothy* 2:3)—because **our faith is a spiritual war against the Devil and all evil. We must also practice our faith like a high performance athlete training for elite competition** (1 *Corinthians* 9:24-27).

If God demands this of us—and **our response is to be half-hearted, what else can we expect that God will do with us when we die**—except *Revelation 3:16*? ("**Because you are lukewarm—neither hot nor cold—I am about to spit you out of my mouth**") After all, he applies EOF to us (= 'you reap what you sow').

Many of the people who slack off spiritually in their lives are emboldened by a <u>misinterpretation</u> **of verses like** *Romans* **11:29 that tell us,**

"God's gifts and his call are irrevocable."

They believe in the doctrine of **'once saved, always saved'**—which is true. Once you are saved—you cannot go to hell. The **salv-** part of the word salvation means **'safe'** in Latin. You are safe from hell. **But you are also not going to go to Living Heaven (=** Paradise) with God. **At best, you will go to Dead Heaven**—after God destroys your soul—along with the majority of humanity who are lost. The **worst case scenario is that you <u>will</u> go to Hell**—if you were never properly saved in the first place. I—personally—would not want to chance spending eternity in Hell because of nuances in the salvation process that I might have gotten wrong.

In any case, this is an unfortunate scenario. **You have unworthy people trying to 'game the system' and sneak past God into heaven on a technicality**. But it does help us understand certain aspects of the EOF law—discussed in *Psalm* 18:26—that we quoted earlier,

"To the devious you show yourself shrewd"

With EOF, God responds to our actions with reciprocity—tit for tat or equality in kind and degree. But if we stoop to evil—God will not follow us down into the moral sewer. **He never abandons the moral high ground of good**. If devious people try to sneak into heaven by deliberately slacking off after becoming saved—he will show himself shrewd. Little do they know there is not just one heaven—but two. **God will cut them off from the heaven they want—Living Heaven—and send them to the heaven they don't want (or even know about)—<u>Dead</u> Heaven**. Some of them in fact, as we saw, might even go to Hell for their efforts. That is God being shrewd.

One thing people have to keep in mind about **EOF—both the physical law and its spiritual counterpart**—is that it is <u>reactive</u>. **It only responds to some <u>earlier</u> initial force or action.** The reason this matters is that some people get confused when they read in various parts of the Bible that God 'hardened' someone's heart. This could be Pharaoh in Egypt who refused to let the Israelites leave the land. Or the Canaanites who resisted the Israelites' conquest of the Promised Land, etc.

But—whoever it is—people might think it is unfair of God to hold them accountable for hardening their hearts, since the Bible itself says that <u>God</u> was the one who hardened their heart. But God only interacts with people by EOF—so this means that **the person with the hardened heart was the one who <u>first</u> hardened their heart against God**. God merely responded back to this initial impulse from the person—in keeping with his EOF law.

It should be kept in mind that **the initial impulse from a person that God responds back to, could be something done earlier in their life; or it could even be some impulse of theirs made <u>before</u> they were even born**—while God was scanning their SDF toward him pre-birth. People always retain their free will to act. But there are consequences for their choices.

With EOF, any good you do 'boomerangs' back to reward you—now or in the future. Likewise, any evil you do 'boomerangs' back to punish you—now or in the future. And this includes having your heart 'hardened'. **You could say that God hardened someone's heart. Or that God's spiritual law of EOF hardened their heart**.

It is the same in the natural world. When someone fires a gun, and the gun recoils, you could say God recoiled the guy's gun. Or you could say it was Newton's 3rd Law of Motion in physics—that God set up. But the guy shooting off the gun, caused the recoil. Likewise, **a person <u>first</u> rejecting God and his purpose in their life—caused the hardening of their heart**.

The only exception to the strict operation of EOF ('you reap what you sow') was when Christ died on the cross for us. *Colossians* 2:13-14 tells us,

"When you were dead in your sins and in the uncircumcision of your flesh,

> God made you alive with Christ. He forgave
> us all our sins, having canceled
> the charge of our legal indebtedness,
> which stood against us and
> condemned us; he has taken it away, nailing it to the cross."

Strictly speaking, **we deserve death for our sins. But by his grace—the undeserved favor that God, in his love for us, chooses to give us—<u>we can escape the death penalty</u> by having faith in his atoning death for us**. [See the **Prayer for Salvation** at the end of this book]

Einstein's Theory of Relativity, E = MC2 and the Christian Gospel

We have already seen that spiritual relativity is—like EOF—one of God's most important laws that he follows when interacting with people. **He judges people only by the level of awareness of good and evil they have, when they commit an act**. Did they know an act was wrong when they did it? If they knew it was wrong—he charges them with sin. If they didn't know—he doesn't. **Young children and animals basically get a full pass on sin for <u>any</u> of their actions**. And even with adults—he lets a lot 'slide'.

Remember the Pharisees in *John* 9:41. They rejected Jesus' teachings and then scoffed at the idea that they were (spiritually) blind for doing so. Jesus told them,

> "If you were blind, you would not be
> guilty of sin, but now that you
> claim you can see, your guilt remains."

When God created our Material World, he established this new, milder relative system of justice given the frailties and limitations of mankind and all the animal species. **They were to be judged only 'relative' or proportionate to their level of awareness. He did this**

out of love for us, following another law—EOF—the spiritual law of proportionality and reciprocity.

As we saw, the laws in God's own Spiritual World are much different. There the much harsher absolute standard of justice prevails. **Spirit beings—angels and demons—have full awareness of God's existence and all his laws**. As a result, a single sin—for any reason—is enough to condemn one to Hell forever with no chance of forgiveness—as happened with the Devil and his demons. This too is proportional justice governed by EOF.

People knew about spiritual relativity early on—because it occurs all throughout the Bible. But scientists discovered its counterpart—physical relativity—only recently in the 20th century.

According to physical relativity, the <u>physical</u> nature of all objects in the material world—including people—is not fixed (= absolute), but relative (= dependent on some other factor). That factor is how fast they are traveling relative to the speed of light—which is 186,000 miles per second.

So take, for example, a 6-foot-tall man. **Strictly speaking, it is wrong to simply say he is 6 foot tall—as if this were an unchanging absolute**. According to physical relativity, his height is variable depending on how fast he is traveling relative to the speed of light. So, if you were to see that 6-foot-tall man hurtling headfirst through space traveling at 87% of the speed of light, you would see that he is now only 3 feet tall. And if you saw him travel at 99.5% of light speed, you would see that he has shrunk even further—now being only a little more than 7 inches tall.

Technically, our 6-foot-tall guy is <u>only</u> 6 feet when he is not moving at all or traveling at very low speeds relative to the speed of light. Since the only speeds we will likely ever encounter in our daily life are very slow ones, we can keep saying he is '6 feet' tall—as if this were an unchanging absolute. But scientists know that the size of physical objects in our world will shrink and expand like this when they travel at speeds close to light speed.

The parallel spiritual law of relativity works like this: it **says that the (moral) nature of an action (= good or bad) is relative**

to (= dependent on) the (spiritual) light in which you view it. If you (genuinely) don't have enough light to know that an action is wrong when you commit it—God <u>won't</u> charge you with a sin for it.

But if you <u>did</u> have enough light to know that something was a sin—and still did it—God <u>will</u> charge you with a sin. We need to be clear: **just because you didn't <u>know</u> something was a sin—doesn't mean that it, in fact, isn't a sin. It is just that God will not <u>charge</u> you with a sin because of your lack of knowledge**. Conversely, it may happen that you may have thought something was a sin—but it turns out it really isn't. God won't charge you with a sin for that either.

Einstein's theory of relativity is described by the **well-known formula E = MC2. This means that the amount of energy (E) an object has, is equal to its mass (M) times the speed of light (C) squared. Light is the fastest thing in the universe** moving at 186,000 miles per second. It consists of 100% energy. **It serves as the sole absolute in our Material World**. Everything else has a nature that is determined by how fast it is traveling relative to light speed. But light is not dependent on anything else for its own nature. It is independent or absolute.

In its role as the only absolute upon which everything else is dependent—**light is the Material World analogue or symbol of God**. God is not dependent on anything; but everything in the universe was created by God and all living objects will stand judgement before God.

The Bible, of course, links God with light throughout. *1 John* 1:5 tells us,

"God is light"

Jesus—the second person of God—says in *John* 8:12,

"I am the light of the world"

King David says in *Psalm* 27:1,

"The Lord is my light and my salvation"

What is special about light is that nothing in the universe can ever approach it. Even if you were to travel at the speed of light—light would still be going 186,000 miles per second faster than you. Light here is said to be an absolute because its speed is fixed at 186,000 miles per second, faster than any other object.

What separates us most from God is that he is 100% holy—and we are not. If God wanted to, he could right now bring us into his presence or come into our world. After all, he is all powerful (**"all things are possible with God"** (*Mark* 10:27). What stops him from doing this is his hatred of sin. **God cannot endure any sin in his presence**. That is why he separates himself from us—unless we are cleansed of our sins by faith in the sacrificial death of Jesus Christ.

Now **every object in the Material World—except light—contains at least some mass—which is basically slowed-down energy. Any mass that an object has—slows its speed down**. Even if something is mostly made of energy, the presence of **even a tiny amount of mass in an object will slow it down so that it cannot reach the speed of light**.

Approaching the speed of light is like approaching God. How? As objects approach the speed of light—the limits of our Material World begin to disappear. Time comes to a halt and the three physical dimensions—length, width and height—disappear (when an object approaches each dimension headfirst). **Things start to look theologically like heaven—the realm of God; it is eternal (= lacking time), everywhere (= limiting physical dimensions fall away) and full of light (= God)**.

It is the mass in us—analogous to sin—that keeps us all from achieving light speed. It is impossible for us—by our own efforts—to ever achieve light speed since it takes literally an infinite amount of energy to push any object with mass in it to light speed. <u>Only an infinite being—God—would have the power to do this for us</u>.

And there we have the Christian gospel: mankind is separated from God by their sin and cannot by their own efforts enter heaven. Only by God's cleansing us of our sin (= mass), can we become holy enough (= pure energy) to enter his presence.

Lesson #4

Don't Push God Away From You

When you become saved—you have God's <u>infinite</u> power at your disposal. But any time we offer resistance to God's will—we sin—and push God away from us in proportion to the severity of the sin.

That is why **humility is one of the <u>most</u> important virtues** you can possess. **It is the <u>absence</u> of resistance to God's will in your life**. The more humility you have—the less you block God's power from working through you. Put another way, **the humbler you are, the more that God's infinite power can work through you—including miracles**. And the more—of course—you will grow spiritually.

Psalm 149:4 tells us,

> **"The Lord delights in his people; he crowns the humble with salvation."**

So powerful is humility that it <u>alone</u>—if properly practiced—can grant you salvation.

How Can Humility Alone Grant You Salvation— If Jesus is the Only Way to God?

This Old Testament verse, written centuries before the time of Jesus, reflects a 'relative' view of salvation. The relative path to salvation is, as we said, for people who lived in a time or place that never knew about Jesus. This includes everyone reading the book of *Psalms* in ancient Israel—hundreds of years before Jesus.

If you sincerely seek to do what is right in your heart, God—in

the person of Jesus—will notice this and come to help you (= EOF). Such **Jesus apparitions**—leading to conversion and salvation—**are a well-known phenomenon**, for example, **in the Muslim world today**. For various reasons—some cultural, some religious—the potential Muslim believer can't seek out Jesus themselves in their society. So Jesus comes to them.

Jesus <u>still</u> is the gatekeeper or only way to God. After all, it is <u>Jesus</u> who comes to these people appearing to them in their spirit—but sometimes visually as well. Jesus in *Matthew* 5:8 says,

"Blessed are the pure in heart, for they will see God."

When Jesus lived on earth, he interacted with people's souls in person. Now he does the same, but—remotely—from heaven. Either way—the result is the same. Jesus is the gatekeeper judging people's sincerity and efforts. To those who are worthy—he will grant salvation.

When you are humble—that is, you seek not to sin against him—God rewards you and draws you closer to him. **If you keep being humble—God will eventually draw you in this way into his very presence. Being in 'God's presence' is the same as 'salvation' and 'heaven'**. Several Bible verses speak to the importance of humility:

"Humble yourselves before the Lord, and he will lift you up."
(*James* 4:10)

The reason James uses the term 'lift you up' is because the term 'humble' literally means to 'lower oneself'. Its opposite—pride—means to 'raise oneself up'. **If you want to raise yourself up spiritually—you do it <u>God's</u> way. You lower yourself before God and <u>he</u> will raise you up**. If you, in your arrogance, try to raise yourself up and exalt yourself—God will humble or lower you as punishment. For *James* 4:6 says,

"God opposes the proud, but gives grace to the humble."

Proverbs 29:23 adds,

"Pride brings a person low, but the lowly in spirit gain honor."

Humility, we said, is <u>non-resistance</u> to God's will. The Bible calls its opposite—pride or resistance to God's will—by the metaphor of being 'stiff-necked' toward God. With this in mind—let us heed the important warning *Proverbs* 29:1 gives us about avoiding pride,

**"Whoever remains stiff-necked after
many rebukes, will suddenly
be destroyed—without remedy."**

The Power of Humility to Make
or Break You Spiritually

We saw that **humility <u>alone</u> can give you salvation**. But it can do even more than that. **With enough of it—it will propel you to the highest levels of heaven**. Yes, **there are degrees of heavenly bliss**. But—if you lack it—<u>you won't even make it to heaven</u>. Jesus illustrates this for us in *Matthew* 18:3-4 using the natural humility of a young child as an example,

**"Truly I tell you, unless you change and
become like little children,
you will never enter the kingdom of
heaven. Therefore, whoever takes
the lowly position of this child is the
greatest in the kingdom of heaven."**

As **an example of the power of humility,** we may look to the example of **Moses** in the Old Testament. God elevated him to one of the highest places spiritually of any person who has ever lived. Why? *Numbers* 12:3 tells us,

> "Now **Moses was a very humble man,**
> more humble than anyone
> else on the face of the earth."

Since God interacts with people through his EOF spiritual law—
**<u>we</u> are the ones who 'short circuit'—by our <u>initial</u> lack of faith—
God's ability to act in our lives with the blessings that** *Psalm* **37:4
tells us God <u>wants</u> to give us,**

> "Take delight in the Lord, and he will give you the desires of
> your heart."

In *Matthew* 13:54-58, Jesus returns to his hometown of Nazareth.
There,

> "He began teaching the people in their synagogue,
> and they were amazed. 'Where did this man get this
> wisdom and these miraculous powers?' they asked.
> 'Isn't this the carpenter's son? Isn't his mother's name
> Mary, and aren't his brothers James, Joseph, Simon
> and Judas? Aren't all his sisters with us? Where then
> did this man get all these things?' And they took
> offense at him. But Jesus said to them, 'A prophet is
> not without honor except in his own town and in his
> own home.' **And he did not do many miracles there
> because of their lack of faith.**"

**The Nazarenes' lack of faith blocked God's ability to work
miracles in their life.** God, of course, had the ability to work those
miracles if he wanted. But, as we said, God chooses to act through
his EOF spiritual law. This law involves: 1) proportionality and 2) God
acts as a <u>reactive</u> force. That is, **people have to <u>first</u> demonstrate
that they have faith that is proportionate to the good thing that
they want God to do for them.**

Many of us today are like the Nazarenes in this regard. **We lack faith at the time we make our requests to God—thus effectively blocking his ability to answer our prayers.** Many people today also make another mistake when praying to God. They ask God for selfish and self-indulgent things that are not the type of prayer that God likes to answer. **God is <u>most</u> likely to answer a prayer if it results in the elevation of the spiritual level of the person / people being prayed for.**

This typically rules out prayers to God to become rich—in earthly terms, at least. Being rich in earthly terms (= money), **pushes you away from God, and <u>lowers</u> your spiritual level with him.** So God is <u>not</u> in the business of answering prayers that do this. But the <u>final</u> answer, of course, as to whether God will answer your prayer or not—is this: does it fit into his complicated global agenda? **If a prayer complements his agenda, he will answer it. If it doesn't, he won't. All answers to prayer, of course, assume that the people praying have the <u>necessary amount of faith</u>—in advance.**

Jesus tells us that it doesn't take a lot of faith—**to literally move mountains.** In *Matthew* 17:20 he says,

> "Truly I tell you, **if you have faith as small**
> **as a mustard seed, you can**
> **say to this mountain, 'Move from here**
> **to there', and it will move."**

Why Does God Care So Much About Our Level of Faith?

Showing faith in God is a form of <u>love</u>. You show you trust his word and are confident he would not lie to you and that he is good to keep his word. These are all positive attributes—**<u>good</u>** things— that you are saying about God. **The good you beam outward at**

God in heaven bounces back to you—by EOF—as good that God gives you in answering your prayers.

So **a lack of humility can block God's power to act in your life—or to even give you salvation**—because 'God opposes the proud'. So can a <u>lack of faith</u> that God can or will answer your prayers. Still **another limiting factor** that we must avoid **is a lack of forgiveness** toward others. Jesus tells us in *Matthew* 6:15,

> **"If you do not forgive others their sins, your
> Father will not forgive your sins."**

The sin that remains in us because God will not forgive us—limits God's ability to answer our prayers and to act through us.

There is a lack of faith people have that prevents God from fully answering our prayers and using us for good in the world. There is also a lack of faith that prevents us from even approaching God in the first place—which is worse. **The doubts people have about God or certain details in the Bible can destroy them spiritually.** So it is important to address some of the main questions people have that keep them from embracing God in the first place.

Many of the doubts non-believers have about God, center around the problem of evil in the world.

Why Does God Allow
Evil in the World?

God—through his careful control of things—has designed everything that happens to people to be spiritually 'good'. Like the sun that continually beams its rays at the earth, or a parent that everyday feeds their children, God continually sends us moral events that we should receive as 'good'.

Even if what happens to us comes in the form of adversity—for example, crime, health issues, job loss, etc.—we should receive it as good. Why? Because **if we receive it as good—it will become good for us.** We saw earlier that this is called **Passive Spirituality**. It is 'good' that God credits us for undergoing undeserved hardship that we accept as 'good'—out of faith in God's goodness in everything. **It is very important that we go through difficult events in life with a cheerful heart.**

This is one of the main ways we earn 'good' to put in our **spiritual 'bank account'** that **we will need** at the end of our lives **on Judgement Day**. The other way is through **Active Spirituality. Active Spirituality,** we saw, **is when you actually do good deeds like leading people to Christ, feeding the poor and helping those in need. The average person is not doing enough active good deeds in their life to earn much spiritual good that way.** So if you haven't earned a lot of spiritual good from Active Spirituality— then you **really** need to earn spiritual good from Passive Spirituality. That is, you need to live a life where you endure a lot of hardship with a good spirit. That is the only way—without a multitude of good deeds from Active Spirituality—to earn a decent amount of good. **But since undergoing adversity is unpleasant— the best thing is to do more active good deeds to boost the amount of good in your spiritual bank account.**

Why do we need 'good' in our spiritual bank account on Judgement Day? This is for the people who are going to Living Heaven. Heaven has different levels with differing degrees of bliss. **Everyone does not have an identical experience of heaven. When you become saved, God resets your spiritual bank account with him to o. When you had sin, this counted as negative amounts of money (= debt)—because sin is debts you owe to God.** *Colossians* 2:13-14 tells us,

"Christ...forgave us all our sins, having canceled the charge of our legal indebtedness, which stood against us and condemned us"

No one with a <u>negative</u> spiritual bank account can get into heaven—because no one with sin can get into heaven. <u>Everyone</u>—before they become saved—has a negative balance. When they become saved—their bank account goes from negative to 0. But **<u>after</u> they become saved—they must do good works to earn <u>positive</u> amounts of spiritual good that will determine their position or status in Living Heaven.**

Once you are saved, **<u>you must earn 'spiritual good' each day</u>** by doing good deeds **(= Active Spirituality)** <u>and</u> enduring hardship with faith as a good thing **(= Passive Spirituality). This is <u>just like</u> you go to work each day to earn <u>earthly</u> money.** This is another example of our earthly world <u>paralleling</u> the spiritual world which God does to teach us spiritual lessons.

So why is there so much evil and suffering in the world? Yes, this is partly because people are allowed—by their God-given free will—to choose evil. **But also—<u>in very large part</u>—<u>because God uses evil in the world as a way for</u> <u>the victims of evil to earn spiritual good that will boost their position in heaven in the next world</u>.**

But notice something important here: **if the 'evil' you experience in life, ends up counting as 'good' for you, is it really still 'evil'?** This is the thing: **God has designed our world so that there is no <u>true</u> evil in it—just <u>apparent</u> evil. True evil is evil that is <u>only</u> evil—with no redeeming good side attached to it. <u>Apparent</u> evil is what we actually have now. Something that is certainly bad—but ends up <u>serving</u> as good—<u>if we accept it with faith as good</u>.**

God has given us the ability <u>to create our own reality</u> in life: if we accept adversity as good through faith—it <u>becomes</u> good for us. But—and here is the warning—if we interpret adversity as evil—because we lack faith—it <u>becomes</u> evil for us. <u>You will lose out on all the spiritual good intended for you by God if you lack faith. Everyone who lacks faith is punished—both in this life and on</u> Judgement Day.

The book of *Job* in the Bible allegorically describes how God uses Passive Spirituality in our lives. Job was a righteous man who endured all manner of trial and adversity in his life. **Yet he stayed faithful to God and believed—all throughout his suffering—that God was good.** Once Job's adversity passed—as it always does—*Job* 42:10 says,

> **"The Lord restored his fortunes and gave**
> **him twice as much as he had before."**

This reflects God's <u>overcompensation</u> with Passive Spirituality: **in return for a season of adversity in this short blip of a life—we get to enjoy a <u>greater</u> spiritual good for endless eternity**.

Historical—and Even Current—Spiritual Error

In ancient times—contemporary with the character of Job—people were unaware of Passive Spirituality. **They assumed that every time someone suffered some (apparent) evil in their life—without exception—it was God's <u>punishment</u> of them for some evil they did.** So all throughout the *Book of Job*, Job's 'friends' keep advising him to just admit the evil he has done so that—with confession—God will relent and his suffering will end. As *Isaiah* 55:9 says—with **God speaking** to people,

> **"As the heavens are higher than the**
> **earth, so are my ways higher**
> **than your ways and my thoughts than your thoughts"**

Even in Jesus' day—hundreds of years later—this error persisted. In *John* 9:1-3, Jesus is asked about this topic,

> "As he went along, he saw a man blind from
> birth. His disciples asked him,

'Rabbi, who sinned, this man or his
parents, that he was born blind?'
'Neither this man nor his parents sinned,'
Jesus said, but this happened
so that the works of God might be displayed in him.'"

The blind man earned spiritual good in his life for being blind, and God used his condition to work good in the lives of others.

Because there is no (true) evil in the world, *Genesis* 1:31 says—after God created the world,

"God saw all that he had made, and it was very good."

Some will object that it was good because this was <u>before</u> mankind's fall brought evil into the world. But the same is true—even <u>after</u> the fall—as *Romans* 8:28 tells us,

"All things work together for good to those who love God"

All things—whether openly good or adversity—serve as 'good' for those who have faith in God.

The Purpose of Life

Remember: this life is only a <u>brief blip</u> compared to the vast backdrop of endless eternity. The purpose of this life is twofold:

1. **Gain entrance to Living Heaven.**
2. **Earn the highest position you can in Living Heaven. Yes, the levels of bliss there <u>are</u> variable. The more 'spiritual wealth' you bring there—the higher your position there and the greater your bliss.**

As an aside, **if your life is <u>not</u> focused on these two goals— you are off task and probably feel a spiritual malaise from God, because you are <u>not</u> doing what you are supposed to.** This is **soul deadening** that we will talk about later.

'Spiritual wealth'—as I term it—is the spiritual analogue or parallel to earthly money. This is the type of wealth you <u>want</u> to accumulate. It brings you <u>closer</u> to God and <u>elevates</u> your position in Living Heaven for eternity. By contrast, Jesus in the Parable of the Sower (*Mark* 4:19) calls earthly money 'deceitful'. It tricks people into chasing after it, instead of <u>real</u> wealth—which is spiritual wealth. Unlike spiritual wealth, **earthly money—kept at levels beyond your basic needs—poisons your relationship with God, diminishes you spiritually and potentially bolsters your position in Hell for eternity.** More on this later.

The Rise and Fall of Civilizations

Spiritual good doesn't just draw an <u>individual</u> closer to God—it draws an <u>entire nation</u> closer to God. Nations with high levels of good moral traits—that lead to high levels of collective spiritual good—will rise and succeed. Nations that are corrupt and widely lacking moral character in their citizens—will fall. Good moral traits include—honesty, discipline, strong work ethic, respect for law and order, loyalty, etc.

What often drags a good nation down—will be the corrosive effects of earthly wealth. Good moral character will typically elevate a nation to prosperity. But wealth—over time—has a corrosive effect on their moral character—and moral decay sets in.

Pretty much inevitably—all cultures weaken and collapse over time under the weight of moral decay. As they weaken, their fall may well be sped along by a conquering enemy who takes advantage of their growing weakness. The ancient Spartans in Greece recognized this problem with wealth. They tried to block this 'law of decay' by strictly limiting how much money each citizen could possess.

People are often confused about their spiritual life before salvation vs. after salvation. We saw earlier that **you can't earn your way to salvation and Living Heaven—because no works of yours are good enough in God's eyes**. **But, by his grace— his undeserved favor for us—he lowers his strict standards and allows people <u>by faith</u> to clear away their spiritual debts to him and become saved.**

But once God has granted you salvation and forgiven your sins—your spiritual 'bank account' with God now stands at 0. **When you were unsaved, your sins were debts that you owed God— equivalent to <u>negative</u> amounts of money.** But now that you are saved—**you need to <u>earn</u> spiritual wealth to put into your bank account. The spiritual wealth you put into your bank account positions you in Living Heaven for eternity. The <u>more</u> spiritual wealth you have—the <u>higher</u> your position there.**

That is one of the reasons—you might have noticed—that **most people become saved at a <u>young or relatively young age</u>. To allow them to build up a reasonable spiritual bank account with God.** Some people—like St. Paul—become saved later at a somewhat older age. In his case, this was because he needed time to build up the necessary amount of Biblical knowledge he would later use as a convert. And God knew he would compensate for his late start by earning extraordinary amounts of spiritual wealth during his Christian ministry.

The other reason most people become saved when they are young, is that—**as people age—they become progressively more Gospel-hardened and sin-entrenched**. Over time, they keep rejecting God's quiet, inner promptings to them to follow him and do what is right. Each time they do this, they—by the EOF spiritual law—push God away from them.

Over many years, **they become so hardened and resistant to God, that it is almost impossible to save any of them. But don't give up praying for unsaved people who are old.** As Jesus said in *Matthew* 19:26, **'with God all things are possible' and they might be one of the exceptions** to the rule.

Physical Laws that Reflect Spiritual Truths

Spiritual **relativity says that the nature of a spiritual event is determined by the 'light' or way you view it—as either good or evil. Physical relativity says that the nature of a physical object is determined by its speed relative to light speed.** Speed is the material world analogue or equivalent of holiness. Physical light is the fastest object in the universe—just as God is the holiest.

A physical object's speed relative to light speed is the equivalent—in spiritual terms—of a person's degree of spiritual light or insight, since holiness confers wisdom. A fast moving object would be equivalent to a person who is very holy—and therefore possesses great spiritual light or insight. As such, physical and spiritual relativity are analogues of each other.

Yet another physical law has relevance here—the **Heisenberg Uncertainty Principle** from quantum physics. It **states that the way we choose to observe physical objects, changes them at the subatomic level**. This is parallel to the way that we view spiritual events—as good or evil—changes their actual nature. The Heisenberg Uncertainty Principle states the following: **if we choose to view the momentum (= speed and direction) of an electron of an atom—its location is unknowable. It effectively blurs out of view. In other words, what we choose to seek out—at the subatomic level of our physical world—comes into focus; what we choose not to seek out—blurs away.**

So, effectively, what the mind seeks out, is summoned into view (= created), while what the mind ignores, blurs away (= disappears). The profound take-away from this is that **our mind can alter the** physical world around us (= reality) by what it chooses to focus on or believe.

The Heisenberg Uncertainty Principle has another tie-in to spirituality. It shows us that **it is <u>impossible</u> for us to ever have <u>full</u> knowledge of the physical world around us. There will always be some uncertainty**. This applies even to mathematics, a field that has 'mathematical certainty'—probably the highest level of proof there is. Even here—**mathematicians have proposed that it is <u>impossible</u> to conclusively prove all their mathematical workings. Some things will just have to be taken on faith.**

All this is the material world parallel to the spiritual world's lack of certainty about God. God has put us—in this lifetime— in a '<u>state of faith</u>' relationship to him for our spiritual well- being—as we saw earlier. God maintains plausible deniability as to his own existence. Our material world was built on the model of the older, eternal spiritual world. **<u>Because there is no certainty about God allowed on a spiritual level among people, there is also no certainty allowed in our material world about anything—even in the fields of math and science.</u>**

Skeptics who demand you <u>prove</u> God exists—are asking for something that is <u>impossible</u>. Some of them—at least—probably know that. **You can only speak of <u>probabilities</u> in our world.** For example, **God <u>most probably</u> exists. How—after all—could you explain all the obvious design, order and complexity in the observable universe?**

It is <u>extremely</u> unlikely (meaning **<u>well</u> beyond many trillions to one in statistical probability**) that our universe could into being— and maintain itself—purely by chance. Saying the universe might always have been there—is just empty speculation devoid of any evidence. There is a far greater likelihood that God exists than this last theory is true.

So any scientist who says they don't believe in God because of lack of evidence—but does believe the universe came into being by chance or was always there—is a fraud. There is no <u>definitive</u> evidence to support <u>either</u> position. We are merely in the realm of probability and faith in both cases. But there is a much greater statistical probability that some supreme God-like power created our orderly universe than that it randomly 'self-assembled' itself. **When science comes to do battle with religion in areas like this— it becomes a religion and ceases to be science.**

The other fraud that 'scientists' try to perpetrate is the Theory of Evolution by Natural Selection—across species. This is a theory that claims mankind arose over time from lower animal forms of life due to changing environmental pressures. Now, to be fair, **on a small scale—within a species—evolution is actually true.**

I say it is true because we can observe certain changes taking place in various plant and animals forms due to some favorable trait they have in a given environment that allows them to out-populate their rivals. **This is real science because it is based on actual, observable evidence and / or experimentation.** We can observe certain plants or animals changing form, function or appearance— based on environmental pressures.

But these environmentally-driven changes are not so great that they cause the various plants or animals to change from their current species—into entirely new species. **We can observe 'micro-evolution' (= small scale) taking place—within plant or animal species. But not 'macro-evolution' (= large scale) in which environmentally-driven changes cause life forms to become entirely new species. When we go from micro-evolution to macro-evolution—we go from real science to a faith-based religion—we will call 'scientism'. We leave behind observable evidence to embrace empty speculation.**

The Theory of Evolution asserts that mankind arose from smaller animal forms of life. It requires as much faith to believe this as it does to believe that the universe in all its order and complexity—just self-assembled by random chance. **The odds against either idea being true are astronomically great—many, many, many times greater than trillions to one.**

So Does Science Contradict Christianity?

No, of course not. God created the Material World as the mirror or parallel of his own Spiritual World. **All the various scientific laws that govern our world—have parallel spiritual laws. This, I would think, would tend to <u>support</u> Christian teachings—not contradict or oppose them**.

The only exceptions are the cross-species theory of evolution (= macroevolution) and the theory that the universe wasn't created by a God-like power—but that everything simply came together by sheer chance. But I don't feel these last two theories are actual science. That is, **they don't have solid evidence—based on experimentation and observation—just empty speculation**. So, as a result, I maintain the view that **science does <u>not</u> contradiction Christianity**.

Observe the intellectual dishonesty of many 'scientists' today who adhere to the scientism of the last two theories. **Christians openly admit that their religion <u>is</u> a religion. That is, it is <u>faith-based with no definitive proof possible</u>**—for the reasons already stated.

But how many scientists do you know who acknowledge that these two theories are actually faith based at their core? Yes, **their subject area is not <u>by definition</u> faith-based**—like a religion— since it seeks to study our observable natural world. **But given the lack of positive evidence for these theories and the great probability against them,** they stubbornly refuse to acknowledge the obvious—that **they are <u>effectively</u> faith-based in actuality, like a religion**. No doubt they fear they will lose credibility with the public if they did so—and were honest.

Some 'scientists' (= pushers of scientism) will **try to deceive the public** when discussing their field. For example, **some evolutionists will boldly assert to the public that evolution is a <u>proven fact</u>**.

By this, they mean specifically **micro-evolution** which basically <u>is</u> proven—as far as anything can be **in our world of limited and non-definitive knowledge**.

But they were appearing in public to promote **macro-evolution—large-scale evolution that crosses species—for which there is no such proof at all.** They used the deceptive cover term of 'evolution' figuring the audience probably wouldn't understand the differences and nuances between micro- and macro-evolution and that they could get away with the deception.

Another deception used to push macro-evolution is when they say that basically <u>all</u> <u>scientists</u> believe in it. When supporters of macroevolution—also called Darwinism—have to resort to telling people that most scientists believe in it—this is <u>an appeal to authority</u>.

Appeals to Authority Are a Good Sign of a <u>Weak</u> Argument

As we saw—**<u>nothing</u> in this world is 100% provable.** But having to stoop to make **an appeal to authority—is something people do when the evidence for their argument is weak or non-existent. People are <u>not</u> convinced by their facts—or they don't have <u>any</u> to show—<u>so they try to bypass facts and evidence</u>.** You don't hear people say 'most mathematicians believe that 2 + 2 = 4' or 'most experts feel that you can't shove a square peg into a round hole'. **These arguments have solid evidence to support them. They don't need appeals to authority.**

But supporters of macroevolution want people to forget about facts. Just simply trust the scientists. This is a faith-based system—just like a religion. The idea behind this kind of appeal to authority is: **why would all the scientists believe in it—if it weren't true?** The accurate, non-politically correct **answer is that they are**

by and large coerced into—at least publically—giving lip-service acceptance of it.

It is possible that a number of scientists may <u>not</u> be aware of how shoddy the evidence actually is for macroevolution. This is especially the case for scientists not directly in the field of macroevolution, but in hard sciences—like physics and chemistry—where the standards of evidence are much higher and they couldn't get away with what macro- evolutionists do.

James Perloff has two good books out on the failings of macroevolution; in terms of the lack of evidence <u>for</u> it—and the considerable evidence <u>against</u> it. They are a shorter introduction to the topic called **The Case against Darwin: Why the Evidence Should Be Examined** and a longer, more in-depth one called **Tornado in a Junkyard: The Relentless Myth of Darwinism**. I recommend them both.

So **do all scientists really believe in macroevolution?** The reality is this. <u>**Scientists are held hostage to their funding sources**</u>. **If they cannot secure funding to carry out their research—they won't be able to <u>do</u> any research. This will cause them to not get tenure—if they work for universities—or they will simply be fired for lack of productivity—if they work for corporations.**

So **scientists live in <u>justifiable</u> fear of saying or doing anything that will cause them to lose funding. Speaking out against evolution—or some other current fraudulent science agenda being pushed—is a great way for a scientist to <u>lose all their funding and destroy their</u> <u>career as a result</u>.**

Why? Because the science power structure wants to push macro-evolution and they control all the significant sources of scientific funding. **The science establishment that pushes the deception of universal support for macro-evolution, counts all the scientists who are too scared to speak out against it or question it— as <u>supporters</u> of it. That way, between the brainwashed or**

agenda-driven pushers of it and those too scared to oppose it—
you have pretty much all scientists accounted for.

And that is also why you will find that **pretty much the only
scientists who <u>will</u> speak out against macro-evolution are of
<u>two</u> types**:

1. **Those who are <u>retired</u>—and don't need the funding
   anymore.**

2. **Those who have <u>already established their reputation</u> in
   the field of science and can't be as easily threatened by a
   cutoff of funding as a result.**

Yet **a third form of deception** regarding macro-evolution is
that when it is taught in schools, the media or scientific venues,
**its supporters will never—on their own—mention any weak
spots or criticisms of the theory** (even recognized scientific ones).
**If supporters never <u>mention</u> there are any problems with the
theory—the public just assumes that there <u>aren't</u> any problems.**

It should not come as a shock that these two fraudulent theories
of scientism—**cross-species evolution and random creation of the
universe—just happen to be the ones that openly contradict the
Bible.**

**The Bible says God created mankind <u>in his own image</u> after
he created the entire universe. The two fake theories were
devised and pushed to the public to try to attack people's faith
in the Bible—and therefore God himself.**

**Macroevolution seemed to offer an alternative explanation
for the origin of mankind and the universe—<u>which didn't need
God or the Bible</u>. <u>It was an important step in weakening the
spiritual level of the Western world and helped pave the way for
the growth of atheism, materialism and immoral self-indulgence
that still plague us today</u>.**

In the early discussions of macro-evolution, the obvious scientific
problems with the theory were ignored. As a result, **the general**

public assumed the arguments behind it <u>must</u> be strong. Also, since major scientific, media and intellectual figures all <u>seemed</u> to offer support— many people climbed on board and accepted the theory.

The propaganda also demonized opponents of the theory: they were **depicted as backwards, ignorant, non-scientific, non-rational or anti-modern. The intellectually insecure fell for it and damaged themselves spiritually with God**. The punishment from God they reaped for being cowardly in this matter during their brief lives—will afflict them for eternity.

Removing God from creation—as macroevolution did—also paved the way for removing God from people's lives and society in general. **With God out of the way, it didn't seem like such a big deal anymore to devalue life: large-scale slaughter in world wars, including civilian populations, killing the young with abortion and the elderly with euthanasia, etc.**

We shouldn't be surprised to see that **many of the forces pushing evolution to the public are very anti-God and anti-religion**. In fact, **an attempt is underway to replace religion— and in particular, Christianity—with another religion: <u>science and evolution</u>. The scientists have become the new high priests: everything they say must be believed—no questions asked.**

The power structure around the globe pushing agendas such as evolution—that are trying to destroy religion—**are beholden to the Devil**. After all, **Jesus calls the Devil 'the god of this world'** (2 *Corinthians* 4:4). In *John* 16:11, he references the Devil as **'the prince of this world'**. In *Luke* 4:5-6, when the Devil is tempting Jesus, we learn,

> **"The Devil took him to a high place and
> showed him all the kingdoms
> of the world in an instant. The Devil
> said to him, 'I will give you all
> the power and glory of these kingdoms.
> All of it has been given to me,**

and I give it to anyone I please."

So **God has** <u>temporarily</u> allowed the Devil to be the ruler of this world. He cannot overrule God or block God from doing what God wants to do. Nor can he <u>force</u> people to do evil against their will. But the <u>Devil can sway people with evil temptations</u> so God can test their faith and their resolve in following him. He has a limited—but very real role to play in earthly affairs. He serves as the focus and director of evil all throughout the world.

The **kingdoms of this world** that the **Devil mentions** to Jesus, **make up today** what I will call the **global Satanic power structure**. The rich and powerful in pretty much every country are beholden—in varying degrees and ways—to the Devil or those who worship the Devil.

A <u>surprising amount</u> of the leadership and upper levels of people in government, business, banking & finance, entertainment, media, education, military, police, science, law and medicine, etc.—are beholden to serving the Devil and promoting evil in the world.

They have made not just figurative—but <u>literal</u> pacts with the Devil—in order to get earthly power, wealth and pleasures. **Such people are put into positions of power and influence on the condition that they pledge their soul to the Devil. They are given strict handlers to make sure they stick to the overall satanic agenda and don't get cold feet or any pangs of conscience while doing their evil deeds.**

These are the people who **push countries into deadly and destructive wars for their own profit. They collapse economies and siphon off wealth from them—all around the world by crooked financial shenanigans. They poison the food, water, soil and air; steal from the poor; corrupt cultures with immoral and anti-God entertainment. They deceive people through their controlled media and school systems. These shield them from what <u>is</u> important, overwhelm them with trivia that <u>isn't</u>, and**

73

deny the ubiquitous Satanic system and agenda taking place in plain sight in front of them.

Just Because Evolution is False—Doesn't Mean Everything in the Bible is <u>Literal</u>

It should be clear by now that the Bible—and especially **the Old Testament—is filled with <u>many</u> instances of figurative imagery that should <u>not</u> be taken literally.** In fact—as we have seen—if you <u>do</u> take many details of it literally, you will arrive at conclusions that are the exact <u>opposite</u> of what God intended.

But I have to briefly address this issue because **the pushers of macroevolution, using propaganda (= deceptive argumentation), have set up fake opponents for themselves called 'Fundamentalists'.** They didn't do this recently—but well over a hundred years ago—about the time they rolled out the idea of macroevolution beginning with Charles Darwin in the 19th century.

These **Fundamentalists were depicted in the media of the time—owned largely by the same forces pushing evolution— as being rabid, Bible traditionalists. According to the popular caricature, they hated all 'science'—like macroevolution—and even modernity itself.**

Their most conspicuous characteristic, however, was that **they supposedly interpreted everything in the Bible <u>literally</u>. One of their main tenets was that God created the world only a mere 6000 years ago** according—they said—to the *Book of Genesis*. **Because they 'knew' this—the claims of evolutionists that the world was much older—<u>had</u> to be wrong since they contradict the Bible.**

First of all, **there is <u>no such thing</u> in the real world as a 'Fundamentalist'—who takes everything in the Bible literally. <u>Everyone</u> acknowledges that many parts of it are figurative.** For example, Jesus says of himself in *John* 10:9 that he is the 'gate' to God that everyone must enter through to reach God. Elsewhere

(*John* 6: 51), he says that he is the 'bread' that came down from heaven. **Nobody thinks that Jesus is literally <u>a gate or literally a loaf of bread</u>**.

Rather, the idea of Fundamentalists is a <u>fake construct</u> created for propaganda reasons. **If you create fake opponents who seem foolish, backward and buffoonish, you—and your ideas—will appear smarter <u>by comparison</u>.** Your argument may not be very strong, but if your opponents seem much worse—people will side with you.

Staging **debates between evolutionists and Fundamentalist proponents of a 6000 year-old world—also had another benefit for the evolutionists. It took the spotlight off the weakness of the theory of evolution, and <u>put everyone's focus on the fake argument of a</u> 6000 year-old world**—that isn't even in the Bible.

As long as people are focused on <u>the weakness of the other guy's argument, they won't even notice how weak your own argument is</u>. And people <u>are</u> surprised to learn how weak the evidence for cross-species evolution really is—because most science is <u>normally</u> very evidence-based and therefore strong. People naturally tend to defer to scientists when they explain their theories.

The idea that some people have that the world is 6000 years old—comes from this. In *Psalm* 90:4, it says that—with God a day is 'like a thousand years'. And God created the world in 6 days—so 6000 years. But saying a day is '<u>like</u> a thousand years' is not the same as saying a day <u>is</u> exactly a thousand years. So this isn't proof.

Mankind came last in the order of creation—reflecting his status as the pinnacle of God's creation. The Bible never says—or cares to say—how much <u>real</u> time has elapsed between the various stages of creation—from the earth to the sea to plants and animals and mankind.

Now—to be fair—it wouldn't surprise me if the history of <u>human civilization</u> weren't much older than 6000 years. But, the point is, the Bible doesn't categorically assert this. And also, **another propagandistic (= fake) aspect of the evolution** debate—deliberately put out to the public—is the notion that if evolution <u>were</u> true, this would completely invalidate Christianity.

<u>None of this is the case</u>. If, hypothetically, mankind <u>did</u> evolve from lower species of animals, he only became <u>modern</u> man when God 'created' him by giving him a soul. This made him aware of God and spirituality and therefore set him apart from all other animals. At that point, human history might be said to have begun and continued to this day.

But—the point is—whether evolution is true or not, has no effect on the validity and reality of Christianity. Nobody cares either way. So believe it if you want. But the Christian worldview—and how this affects you—is unchanged and real. Do <u>not</u> be deceived.

The Popular Depiction of the Devil is Wrong

Some people find the figure of the Devil with horns, a pitchfork and tail—as a real stumbling block to believing in God and the Bible. This is certainly understandable—because it does seem absurd. The good news is—<u>none of it is true</u>. **The Bible never physically describes what the Devil looks like**. For that matter, nor does it describe what God looks like.

When Christianity spread outside of ancient Israel to non-Jews of the neighboring Greco-Roman world, this lack of clarity about what the Devil looked like—was a problem. The prior religion of these new converts to Christianity was the pagan religion of the 12 Olympian gods—such as Zeus, Apollo and Athena. In this religion, there was no question about what all the gods looked like—because there were statues, paintings and drawings of them everywhere. So people had a clear image in their mind about what each of the gods looked like—or was supposed to look like.

When they converted to Christianity, they noticed there weren't any pictures or images of God—or even of the Devil. This was because of God's commandment not to have any such images. So—probably unconsciously—**new converts began to visualize the Devil as the god Pan** of their former religion. **Pan was a satyr or ½ man, ½ goat.** He was <u>not</u> really like the Devil of the Bible in all his evil and malice. But he was the closest thing to the Devil the Greco-Roman religion had. He was a prankster. While he watched over his flocks in the remote countryside, he would often become bored. So when he saw an occasional traveler walk by—he would enjoy sneaking up behind them and yelling 'boo' to scare them. **That is where we get the word 'panic' from.**

Since Pan was part goat, he had horns, a tail and cloven-hoofs. Because he was a shepherd, he had a pitchfork to fight off any potential wolves who threatened his flocks. Amazingly, this loose, informal linkage of Pan from Greek and Roman mythology with the Devil endured. **People even <u>today</u> picture the Devil this way—even though it is nowhere to be found in the Bible.**

The problem is, some people use this false and absurd depiction of the Devil as a reason **not to believe in the Devil—or in the Bible or Christianity.** But even more: **if people don't believe in the Devil (= Satan), they won't believe the global power structure is organized and <u>Satanic</u> in nature. They will just assume** that **all the problems** we have in the world—as we approach Armageddon—**are due to ordinary selfishness of rulers or powerful people—nothing more.**

Some people—even if they don't believe in a Devil with horns and a pitchfork—still find the <u>Biblical</u> depiction of the Devil as absurd. They say, the Devil knows that God exists and he clearly sees that God is more powerful than he is. Why, then, does he devote himself to the obviously suicidal course of trying to thwart God's will? **Surely he must know that his future involves nothing more than eternal punishment in Hell? Why choose such a preposterous and self-destructive destiny for oneself?**

Even more, the Devil doesn't have any power to act on his own.

He must first ask God for <u>permission</u> to do anything. Jesus in *Luke* 22:32 says to the apostle (Simon) Peter,

> "Simon, Simon, Satan has asked to sift
> you as wheat. But I have prayed
> for you, Simon, that your faith may not fail."

So God monitors and has full control over the Devil's activities among mankind. The Devil may attempt to do something—but God must first <u>allow</u> it—or it will never take place. The Devil is kept on a very restrictive leash. Compared to God, the Devil is powerless. **His ultimate function is merely that of a servant who <u>unwittingly</u> does the work that God needs done in the world. He is <u>only</u> allowed to engage with mankind in ways that ultimately serve the will of God.**

God allowed the Devil and his band of angels to rebel because he needed someone to play the role of <u>tempter of evil</u> in the world. He knew that mankind, who he was about to create, would be given free will to choose to do good—or evil. Before the creation of the world, he foresaw by looking at people's collective SDF that many would choose to do evil.

He then designed <u>beforehand</u> how all of life in the world he was about to create would play out. Everyone would act out—in exact proportion—all the good or evil God saw beforehand in his mind's eye that they were disposed or inclined to do. **God would naturally play the role of the one who encourages people to do good. But he needed someone to play the role of the one who encourages people to do evil**. He, of course, couldn't play that role because *James* 1:13 tells us,

> **"God cannot be tempted by evil, nor does he tempt anyone"**

So the <u>Devil</u> would be the 'sucker' who would unwittingly play this role of the foil to God—who is fated to lose in the end. In the same way, when God was going to deliver the children of

Israel out of slavery in Egypt—he needed a foil. So he raised up Pharaoh to be the sucker.

Mind you—he didn't victimize the Devil. He foresaw that the Devil had a disposition or desire to do evil—and so accommodated his wishes. He didn't lure someone who had no inclinations at all to do evil and burden him with this role.

It is not hard to understand how you get the Devil and Pharaoh to play suicidally stupid roles in history. **Whenever anyone sins—whether people or a created angelic being like the Devil—a spiritual delusion sets in and they lose discernment and become foolish. The bigger the sin—the bigger their delusion**. Given the magnitude of the Devil's sin—God sent him an industrial-strength delusion: up is down, left is right—and he has a real good chance of overthrowing God.

2 Thessalonians **2:11-12** touches on this topic. It describes those lost souls who will be foolish enough to try to take on God at the Battle of Armageddon. This will happen in the coming days of **the Antichrist—the third in the trifecta of suckers throughout history after the Devil and Pharaoh.**

> **"God will send them a powerful delusion**
> **so that they believe the lie,**
> **in order that judgement may come**
> **upon all who have disbelieved**
> **the truth and delighted in wickedness."**

Is God Fair?

Jews vs. Non-Jews

Does God today unfairly elevate Jews over non-Jews? No. But since there is so much confusion about this topic, we must first explain what we mean by this and give some background information.

The <u>ancient</u> Jews (= pre-70 AD) were different from the rest of mankind—past or present. The reason for this goes back to their special role as the 'Chosen People' of God and the spiritual teacher and light to the world. Their close familiarity with God was a result of the fact that **God's presence literally dwelt among them**. God's proximity to them uniquely affected their spiritual status and helped drive much of their subsequent history.

St. Paul in *Romans* 2:9-11 describes their special status with God,

> **"There will be trouble and distress for**
> **every human being who does evil;**
> **first for the Jew, then for the Gentile [=**
> **non-Jew]; but glory, honor and**
> **peace for everyone who does good; first**
> **for the Jew, then for the Gentile.**
> **For God does not show favoritism."**

From this, we see that **God 'weights' the rewards—good and bad—for the deeds of Jewish people differently from those of the rest of mankind. That is, when a Jew does something good—** it counts for <u>more</u> than the same deed that a non-Jew does. Likewise, anything bad that a Jew does—counts for <u>more</u> than the same deed that a non-Jew does. In other words, <u>**God has 'raised the stakes' spiritually for everything the Jews do—for good or for bad**</u>.

The obvious question then becomes: **how can God be said to <u>not</u> practice favoritism—when his treatment of the Jews would seem to be the very definition of favoritism?** The answer is this: God interacts with mankind according to the EOF-based spiritual law found in *Luke* 12:48,

"To whom much is given, much will be demanded"

The equally true reverse corollary to this would be 'to whom little is given, little is expected'. God applies this spiritual law to <u>all</u> mankind—Jew and non-Jew alike.

What creates a special status for the Jews—is that God

'dwelt' among ancient Israel. **The Jews had a greater <u>knowledge</u> of him and his requirements. More is expected of those who have a greater knowledge of right and wrong.** That is why we fault a 20-year old for a temper tantrum in public more than a 2-year old. Same offense—different consequence. The misdeed of the person with greater knowledge—the 20-year old—was judged to be worse because of their greater knowledge.

So greater knowledge of God explains why Jews have all their <u>evil</u> deeds count for more with God than other peoples. But why do their <u>good</u> deeds also count for more with him? This is for a different reason. **The <u>ancient</u> Jews—as part of ancient Israel— are unique in world history because God 'co-opted' their history in ancient times to illustrate spiritual principles to mankind. By 'helping' God to teach the world spiritual principles—through being coopted—it is like you are doing God a favor that he rewards you for.**

How the Israelites' History Teaches Us Spiritual Principles

We saw earlier—in a basic way—how the history of ancient Israel illustrates how salvation works for mankind. The Israelites start out in slavery in Egypt. **The Israelites represent all of mankind who—because of their sins—are condemned to Hell.** The 'iron-smelting furnace' of Egypt (*Deuteronomy* 4:20) symbolizes the fires of Hell—while their physical slavery symbolizes every man's slavery to sin. Jesus tells us in *John* 8:34,

"Very truly I tell you, everyone who sins is a slave to sin."

God frees the Israelites from slavery through the actions of Moses. <u>Moses is a Christ</u> figure who overcomes the powerful opposition of Pharaoh—the ruler of Egypt who vows not to let the Israelites go. <u>Pharaoh represents the Devil</u>. Once freed, the

Israelites wander in the Sinai Desert for 40 years. This represents people's normal lifetime after they become saved. That is, it is filled with adversity, trials, temptations and questioning God about why their life is the way it is.

As an aside—**the number 40 in the Bible symbolizes any period of adversity or trial**. The Israelites wander for 40 years, Jesus is tempted by the Devil for 40 days—and the rains of the Great Flood in Noah's day lasted 40 days and 40 nights.

Those Israelites who rebel against God in the desert—are put to death by God. These people **symbolize all those among mankind that <u>God sends to Hell</u>—<u>about 6%</u>**. After 40 years, it is time to enter the Promised Land—which is a symbol of Living Heaven. Later, after they settle the Promised Land, the 12 tribes of Israel split into two entities: 2 tribes become the Kingdom of Judah, and the remaining 10 tribes keep the name Israel.

The 10 tribes of Israel are permanently expelled from the land (= they symbolize all those people among mankind—<u>about 77%</u>—who will <u>end up in Dead Heaven</u>). The 2 tribes of Judah are briefly expelled from the land—but are then able to return. So they manage to <u>stay</u> in the Promised Land. **These 2 tribes—Judah and Benjamin—symbolize <u>those people who will go to Living Heaven</u>—<u>about 17%</u>**.

This long narrative story (spanning <u>several books</u> in the Bible) that symbolizes mankind's salvation statistics—can be briefly summarized by a mere <u>two verses</u> in *Proverbs*—**which are some of the <u>most important</u> in the entire Bible,**

> **"The upright will inhabit the land, and
> the blameless will remain
> in it; but the wicked will be cut off from the land, and the
> unfaithful will be uprooted."**
> **(*Proverbs* 2:21-22)**

This means that the righteous—in Christ—will <u>get</u> to Living Heaven. Those who <u>stay</u> faithful to God—will be able to <u>remain</u>

in Living Heaven. But the wicked will <u>never even get to Living Heaven in the first place</u>. (They will probably end up in Hell— possibly Dead Heaven for the less serious offenders). <u>This last point is key: those who made it to Living Heaven—by being saved—but who later proved unfaithful, will be expelled from Living Heaven into Dead Heaven</u>.

Notice how the <u>same</u> spiritual truths can be expressed in the Bible in different ways:

1. By long symbolic narrative stories
2. By the condensed wisdom of a proverb

Co-opting involves God controlling your life. So it is very invasive of your freedom. In a broad sense, God—as we saw—controls the events that happen in <u>everyone's</u> life. And, if you look hard enough, you can find spiritual principles illustrated in <u>everyone's</u> life. That is why people value the study of history: you can learn from other people's successes and failures—from the safe distance of history.

But the co-opting of ancient Israel takes this much further. <u>Ancient Israel's history mirrors spiritual teachings in far greater detail than any one individual's life</u>. St. Paul was able to 'mine' numerous Old Testament stories for their symbolic spiritual value hundreds of years later for Christians of his own day.

God's co-opting can also involve just <u>individuals</u>. **Jesus' life was the classic example of this. He was born so that his life would live out all the Old Testament messianic prophecies. These included those of the Suffering Servant (*Isaiah* 53), the sacrificial lamb (*Exodus* 12) and the scapegoat (*Leviticus* 16).**

John the Baptist's life offers another example of God's co-opting. John lived a solitary existence in the Judean wilderness for years as he fulfilled his role as the herald of the Messiah Jesus. His life was pre-determined for him because he had to live out the prophecy of *Isaiah* 40:3,

> "A voice of one calling: 'In the desert
> prepare the way for the Lord,
> make straight in the wilderness a highway for our God'"

After his ministry to Israel that prepared the way for Jesus, John's life ended with his being imprisoned and beheaded for his faith.

Anyone whose life God co-opts—whether individually or collectively—is richly rewarded by God for this. Jesus says of John in *Matthew* 11:11,

> "Truly, I tell you, among those born of
> women there has not risen anyone
> greater than John the Baptist"

As for Jesus, *Philippians* 2:9 tells us, "**God has highly exalted him**". <u>**In the same way, God rewarded the ancient Israelites for his co-opting of their history to serve his purposes**</u>.

So the ancient Jews' spiritual status differs from that of non-Jews for these two reasons. They are held more accountable for any <u>evil</u> they do—because they had greater <u>awareness</u> of God and his will. They dwelled <u>in his presence</u>—unlike all other people on earth. They are rewarded to a greater degree for any <u>good</u> they do—because God is rewarding them for co-opting their history.

The fact that ancient Jews faced heightened judgement for any evil they do, is what lies behind Jesus' response to the Syro-Phoenician woman who asks him to drive out a demon that her daughter has. Jesus tells her in *Mark* 7:27-29,

> "'First let the children eat all they want,' he
> told her, 'for it is not right to take
> the children's bread and toss it to the dogs.'
> 'Lord,' she replied, 'even the dogs

under the table eat the children's crumbs.'
Then he told her, 'for such a reply,
you may go; the demon has left your daughter.'"

Because the woman is <u>humble</u> in response to his words—Jesus <u>does</u> grant her request. The children are the Jews and their bread is spiritual teachings. Jesus knew the Jews would face harsher judgement from God if they did not do what is right. **Non-Jews—like the Syro-Phoenician woman—would <u>not be held as accountable</u> before God as the Jews because they had much less awareness of God's will.**

So Jesus correctly points out the situation: it <u>would</u> be wrong to take time away from teaching people who face <u>greater</u> accountability before God—in order to attend to a person facing <u>much less</u> accountability. **But his words <u>are</u> harsh—because he is testing her. Someone lacking humility would be triggered by them—as many of us today are—2000 years later.**

But because the woman <u>didn't get upset</u> with Jesus—but <u>humbly</u> accepted his words—he granted her wish. This reaffirms what we said earlier about the **power of humility to win you great favor from God. We should <u>all</u> practice it—just like the Syro-Phoenician woman**.

One final note about co-opting. <u>If you follow God when he co-opts you, he will reward you</u> for this. <u>If you fight against God—</u>like the Devil and Pharaoh did—he will <u>still</u> co-opt you—but <u>not</u> give you any reward. So 'play ball' with God—if he wants to co-opt your life. You—or the Devil—have no power before God. He can do <u>whatever</u> he wants. So be humble before God. Always.

Many Christians Today Are Greatly In Error about the Jews

Jews <u>today</u> are <u>very different spiritually from ancient Jews</u>. <u>Ancient</u> Jews, we said, had heightened levels of spirituality—both for good and bad. God counted any 'good' they did as greater than the same good that a non-Jew did. This was God rewarding ancient Jews for co-opting their history.

But **God stopped co-opting the Jews' history in <u>ancient</u> times**. No Jew today—two thousand years later—has had their history co-opted. So **Jews today <u>don't</u> have any 'weighting' of their good deeds as greater than other people's anymore. They are <u>just like everybody else</u> in this regard**.

Likewise, Jews today—whether in Israel or not—no longer dwell in the 'presence of God'. So they <u>no longer</u> have any greater knowledge or awareness of God—than any other people. So God does not weigh any 'evil' they do—as worse than that of any other people—as he used to. <u>Since modern Jews no longer have any heightened levels of spirituality—they are just the same before God as any other people on earth. There is nothing special about them.</u>

But people continue to say that Jews today are the **'Chosen People' of God**. But this term—referencing the 12 Tribes of <u>ancient</u> Israel, which includes the Jews—comes from the <u>Old Testament</u>. **We saw in our discussion of wealth and the Patriarchs like Abraham—that Old Testament language is very different from New Testament language. The <u>exact opposite</u> in fact. We were able to establish this rule of interpretation:**

<u>Literal</u> and <u>physical</u> in the OT = <u>figurative</u>
and <u>spiritual</u> in the NT

God's 'Chosen People' are <u>not</u> in fact <u>literal</u> Israel—the ancient nation of Israel who were physically circumcised—but <u>spiritual</u> Israel—that is, Christians. Christians are <u>spiritually</u> circumcised in that they—at God's prompting—have set themselves spiritually apart from the rest of the nations. They have set aside their earthly nature to follow God's spiritual path in life. St. Paul tells us in *Romans* 2:28-29,

"A person is not a Jew who is one only
outwardly, nor is circumcision
merely outward and physical. No, a person is a Jew who is one
inwardly; and circumcision is circumcision
of the heart, by the Spirit"

Paul calls the church in *Colossians* 3:12, **'God's chosen people'**.
1 *Peter* 2:9 tells believers,

"You are a chosen people, a royal priesthood, a holy nation,
God's special possession"

So the <u>real</u> Jews—the Chosen People—are those who have undergone a <u>spiritual</u> circumcision of the heart; that is, the spiritual transformation of salvation by the Holy Spirit through faith in Christ that all (real) Christians have gone through. It is possible, of course, to be a member of <u>literal</u> Israel and <u>spiritual</u> Israel at the same time. Jesus' Apostles, St. Paul and many of the earliest Christians held this duel status.

Some people even claim that Jews today are spiritually different from all other peoples on earth. They claim that <u>only</u> Jews <u>don't</u> need to find salvation through Christ because God has simply chosen them—for some unspecified reason. But Paul—quoting <u>Jewish</u> Old Testament scriptures—in *Romans* 3:10-12 casts doubt on this,

"There is no one righteous, not even one; there is no one who understands; there is no one who seeks God. All have turned away, they have together become worthless; there is no one who does good, not even one."

If the Jews' own infallible Old Testament scriptures say <u>everyone</u>—including Jews—are morally worthless, why is it, then, that God would choose you? Just asking. Of course, this is all heresy. Jews—like everyone else—are sinners who can <u>only</u> find salvation through Jesus Christ. If not, their fate will be to end up in

Hell or Dead Heaven forever. It is their free will choice. They are <u>the same</u> as everyone else.

God did <u>not</u> choose ancient Israel because they were so much <u>better</u> spiritually than everybody else. This is the fallacy. Rather, they were chosen because they are <u>just as bad as everyone else</u>. The ancient Jews, as a whole, were <u>average</u> people spiritually in terms of their salvation statistics—though they had certain outstanding individuals such as Abraham, Moses and Elijah. **It is precisely because the Jews <u>were</u> average—just like every other nation—that other peoples can relate to them and learn from them. The struggle of ancient Israel to find salvation with God— is the spiritual struggle of <u>every</u> nation and individual.**

Something else problematic you are likely to find among 'church people' these days—is a bumper sticker referencing *Genesis* 12:3. In this verse, God is speaking to <u>one man</u>—and just one man—the faithful patriarch Abraham,

"I will bless those who bless you, and whoever curses you I will curse; and all peoples on earth will be blessed through you."

Next to the Bible verse on the bumper sticker, there is the flag of the modern-day, man-made, political state of Israel. In the original quote, **God's promises were to Abraham—and Abraham alone**. Yes, Abraham will become the father of a great nation. But God never said—either <u>in this verse or anywhere else in the Bible</u>—**that this 'blessing and curse reciprocity' will <u>also</u> be extended to that nation that comes from him. So it is inaccurate and inappropriate to link Abraham's blessing to <u>all</u> of ancient Israel.**

The blessing also only makes sense in regard to Abraham. He remained faithful to God to his dying day. Ancient Israel did not. **God <u>permanently expelled</u> from the Promised Land 10 of the 12 Tribes of Israel for their sins**. They were forever lost to history— becoming known as 'The 10 Lost Tribes'. The remaining 2 tribes were likewise expelled in the so-called Babylonian Captivity. They returned to the land—only to later be <u>permanently expelled</u> after two failed revolts against Rome. <u>**Faithful**</u> **people like Abraham would be the logical recipients of God's blessing—not people who earn his wrath and punishment**.

If it is inappropriate to link Abraham with <u>ancient</u> Israel— it is even more inappropriate to link him to <u>modern</u> Israel. At least ancient Israel was founded by God. Modern Israel wasn't. Even Jewish tradition said that it would be God's <u>Messiah</u> who would restore the Jews to the land of Israel. After getting tired of waiting for him—some Jews took matters into their own hands. **So Israel was founded by men who ignored God**.

It was also the Messiah who—once the Jews were back in Israel—was supposed to rebuild the Temple, restore animal sacrifice and re-establish the ancient Sanhedrin that all existed in Jesus' day. Again, tired of waiting on God to act, men in Israel today have begun these tasks to recreate the atmosphere of ancient Israel. Instead of the Messiah doing these things—once he comes—the viewpoint is <u>reversed</u>: if the Jews today can do these task <u>themselves,</u> then that will <u>cause</u> the Messiah to return right away.

Doing things like rebuilding the Temple and restoring animal sacrifice, doesn't just recreate the atmosphere of ancient Israel. It can also be seen—especially by Christians—as opposing or undoing the work of Christ. Christ did away with continuous animal sacrifice for sins and priests going into the Temple. **Christ— in dying for our sins—made a once-for-all-time sacrifice for our sins. Likewise, a priest doesn't need to enter the Temple for us— because we have the Holy Spirit of God dwelling in the temple of our hearts**.

Some Jews feel that restoring animal sacrifice and rebuilding the Temple are things that will please their Messiah and cause him to return. **Such things will also have the effect of (seemingly) undoing Jesus Christ's works or being against Christ—or anti-Christ**. Can the non-Jewish world speculate in our hearts who this awaited Jewish Messiah might really be? And if the Jews are right that these building projects will speed the coming of their Messiah— can Armageddon be far off?

And if some of these speculations are correct—what does it say about the level of spiritual discernment among many in today's churches that they are praising a country that is awaiting such a Messiah?

Beware Satanically-Infiltrated Churches

Hebrews 10:25 encourages believing Christians not to give up meeting together—in churches. The reason is obvious: meeting with fellow Christians can bolster our faith, help hold us accountable in our walk with God, help us in time of need and provide us with a ready supply of friends and potential mates for marriage.

The problem is that many churches today are deficient in doctrine or practice—or both. Too often they are places where you will find yourself deceived—or at least not getting the kind of spiritual help you need and are looking for. Why is this? Because **the Devil has long targeted churches in order to destroy them from the inside.**

Infiltrating and Corrupting Churches is a <u>Major</u> Goal of the Devil

Corrupting churches—the lifeblood of Christian believers—is an obvious, top-level goal of the Devil. But Satanic infiltration of the church isn't new. It has been around pretty much from the beginning. **Where there is good, evil seeks to infiltrate, subvert and destroy. Churches—as organized centers of good in a community—are obvious targets.**

The **Satanic power structure** using their **financial, political and media influence** can **insert corrupt priests or pastors into existing** churches. Or subvert the leadership of a church denomination—and get them under their sway. Then they can begin pushing an agenda that both subverts traditional Christian teachings and also introduces Satanic ideas covertly.

But it is usually easier to simply start your own church so you can furnish its pastor. Then give the pastor expensive television contracts and promote him heavily—and favorably—in your controlled media.

I say—favorably—because the mainstream media is told by their—real—owners to always give hostile treatment toward authentic traditional Christianity. Someone looking to push heresies or introduce bizarre deviations from traditional doctrine or practice, will however be favorably treated.

Sometimes the Satanists have started not just their own individual churches—but even their own denominations. Or they have induced groups within existing denominations to break away and form their own new denominations that they can then infiltrate and control.

Once they have their people in place on the inside—as priests, pastors or in the leadership of churches—they can then begin to subvert traditional Christian teachings and introduce new Satanic ones as well. Of course, Satanic infiltrators will never openly admit to being Satanic. They will play the role of loyal Christian traditionalist—even as their every action clearly subverts every tenet of real Christianity.

One example of a Satanic doctrine being pushed to the public through infiltrated churches—is the so-called Prosperity Gospel. Jesus told people not to build up earthly treasures for themselves—but spiritual treasures instead that will bring them great spiritual rewards in the afterlife.

Ignoring these clear words of Jesus—the founder of Christianity—these religious frauds push the exact opposite view—just like Satan does. Satan always inverts the truth (= turns it upside down). So when the error in a teaching is not just a little off—but 180 degrees diametrically opposed (= upside down)—it is not likely to be an innocent mistake.

There are a number of sins today—things that God in the Bible openly calls 'abominations'—that clergymen or religious leaders in various churches either want to allow or have <u>already</u> allowed. And this shows that we do not have a genuine, spirit-filled church of God anymore. Rather, it is a spiritually-dead, crypto-Satanic, church of men. **Men—regardless of their status in the world—do <u>not</u> have the power to change God's eternal truths.**

God, for his part, says in *Malachi* 3:6,

"I the Lord do not change."

Likewise, in *Hebrews* 13:8 we read,

"Jesus Christ is the same yesterday today and forever."

So **God <u>and his truth never changes</u>. What was once an abomination, still is today, and will always be one**. Regardless of what men say.

The <u>worst</u> sin that the church long forbid—but then reversed itself to permit because of Satanic infiltration—is usury. Usury originally meant charging someone <u>any</u> interest on loans. Today, they have **changed the definition of the word** to charging **<u>'excessive'</u>** interest.

They did this to cover for the fact that **people can <u>still</u> read in their Bibles God's commands <u>not</u> to practice usury with people in your own society. People might begin to ask why they allow usury today—if God clearly forbid it. But by changing its definition—as they did—they can then say that usury today is something <u>different</u> than what the Bible was talking about.** This is pure Satanic deception that has gone over most people's heads today—even Christian believers.

Speaking of the Devil, Jesus in *John* 8:44 says,

"There is no truth in him. When he lies,
he speaks his native language,
for he is a liar and the father of lies."

The Devil lied to Adam and Eve in the Garden of Eden and he has been lying ever since. Today he lies to us all through his followers in the Satanic power structure who own the largest media around the world. Mind you—they don't have to lie about <u>everything</u>. They don't lie—for example—about sports scores, weather forecasts (which—if wrong—are not intentionally so), human interest stories or new Hollywood movies appearing in theaters. Because the media are honest in these various areas, they build credibility with people so that when they <u>do</u> have to push a Satanic agenda—such as starting an unjustified war—people will believe them.

<u>Most</u> people's world view is full of Satanic deception. Take the example of usury. Many people have been taught to believe that it is a <u>good</u> thing—even necessary—if we want to have a successful commercial economy. Most people don't know that God and the early church banned usury because of the harm it does to a society. **It allows one group of people—the bankers—to acquire exorbitant wealth at the expense of the rest of society—especially the poor.**

It has allowed a class of the super-rich to largely take control of the world. At the end time, these very people—whose religion is Satanism—will attempt to usher in the Antichrist. Jesus called the Devil the 'god of this world'. When Satan tempts Jesus, he offers him all the kingdoms of the world—because, he says, they have been given to him and <u>he can give them to anyone he</u> <u>wants</u>. **That's why the religion of the super-rich and powerful** <u>is</u> **Satanism.**

Newcomers into this system are given great wealth and power because they pledge to worship the Devil and serve their Satanic handlers in pushing the global Satanic agenda. **Surprisingly many ordinary people have literally—not just figuratively—sold their soul for a chance to obtain temporary earthly wealth and power.**

Even though the Bible is very clear about <u>Satanic control</u> of the world—many people today will be skeptical. This is because they have been conditioned to accept a certain worldview—<u>by the world</u>. This worldview scoffs at the notion of Satanic control. In fact, many people today say they <u>don't even believe</u> there is a Devil or Satan.

This is not the case, however, with **the super-rich and powerful.** They **are quite certain there <u>is</u> a Devil.** In fact, when they attend their various elite secret retreats, they will bring along Satanist priests to conduct their Satanic ceremonies. People who are skeptical of all this—lack spiritual discernment. **They have been deceived by the world (= lying Satanic world system) into accepting a false view of the world.**

Others are simply too <u>cowardly</u> to believe in all this. It is more comforting for them to believe the lie that there is no Devil and no Satanic world system pushing us all to Armageddon. Because it scares them to believe in the Devil—they won't. The cowards falsely believe they can avoid any responsibility before God for fighting evil—by simply saying they deny that evil, the Devil and the Satanic world system exist.

The *Book of Revelation* 21:8 tells us that at the end of the world—after Armageddon—there will be a time of reckoning for <u>all</u> people regarding their deeds in this life,

> "But **the cowardly,** the unbelieving, the
> vile, the murderers, the sexually
> immoral, those who practice magic arts,
> the idolaters and all liars—they
> **will be consigned to the fiery lake of burning sulfur"**

Notice how **the <u>first</u> group mentioned—of those who will be thrown into the Lake of Fire—are the cowards.** This group was uppermost in the author's mind as to who deserves this. This is because so many <u>ordinary</u> people fit into this category. **Evil would <u>not</u> flourish today—as much as it does—without so many** ordinary people who are cowards—both inside and outside the church—letting it flourish, by not resisting it. If you are one of these people: things will not end well for you with God if you keep doing this.

Another non-Biblical, false doctrine—spread courtesy of Satanically-infiltrated churches today—**is the Rapture**. There are variations to this belief, but in essence it states that **God will miraculously whisk believers away—from earth to heaven—just before persecution and the threat of evil will harm them.** This appeals to the sensibilities of cowards who don't want to suffer any pain in life. But it has its origin in the pit of Hell.

The problem with this doctrine is that it depicts God as acting in a way that is completely contrary to how he acts in the Bible. As we saw with the Prosperity Gospel, whenever a teaching is—not just a little wrong, but 180 degrees, diametrically opposed to the Bible—it is of Satanic origin. It is Satanic inversion.

So Much of What the Average Person Today Believes—is Satanic Misinformation & Lies

This is true both for religious matters and secular information. **The banker Satanists—through their agents—have installed popular televangelists, individual ministers in churches, the top leadership of a number of denominations, set up churches and denominations and even paid for entire Bible translations—all to deceive people.**

Just For the Record:

When I use the term 'banker-Satanist', I am not—of course—talking about low or mid-level employees at a local bank—such as a bank teller or branch manager. Rather, I mean elite people in the highest echelons of the field who have attained great wealth and influence from their position.

So just because it is a priest or minister who does something—**doesn't** mean it is always good. He could very easily be working for the other side—the Devil**. In fact, priests or other clergymen can be a good way to spread evil in a community. Individuals with known sexual vices or other criminal inclinations, can be installed in a church as priests. They can then be let loose to victimize people in a community.

This creates a lot of evil which Satanists delight in. And if the offending priest gets caught—this can be good too. You use your control of the media to highly publicize the corruption of the offenders. This has the good result—if you are a Satanist—of the public becoming very demoralized with organized religion—or any religion at all.

If you were an evil but shrew Satanist, you could take steps to protect offending priests on their crime sprees that victimized people over a period of many years. If caught in one church—quietly move the priest to another. And then a third, etc. Collusion between church leadership and a rogue individual priest makes for a better story—for the Satanists—when the public hears of it.

People never suspect that Satanists—acting behind the scenes—are instigating so many of the problems in society today. So the real culprits get away scot-free and things never change. **People need to be more aware and have more discernment—if we are ever to stop the criminality and misinformation.**

On Judgment Day, God will judge us all by our spiritual bank account. This consists of all the good deeds we did for others (= Active Spirituality or AS) and all the undeserved adversity sent by God that we endured with faith as good (= Passive Spirituality or PS). People with **negative** bank accounts (= the unsaved in

Jesus) **will go to Hell**. God wants us all to possess <u>as much spiritual good as possible</u>—so we will get the best positions in heaven.

All the greatest people of faith <u>in the past</u> did great good deeds in the world (= high AS) <u>and</u> suffered a lot of undeserved adversity (= high PS). Think of Jesus dying on the cross, John the Baptist being beheaded, Paul and 11 out the 12 Apostles dying violent deaths.

Now along come the 'Rapture' people who say that God will 'save' you from all the pain and suffering you would otherwise experience as a martyr for your faith. **But—in doing this for you— you will lose all the high PS you would have obtained by being a martyr. And you will end up with a much <u>lower</u> place in heaven for eternity as a result. Is this a good thing? No. That is why God <u>never</u> does this. It is not in your best spiritual interests. That is why he never did that with all the saints in the past—and not with his own Son, Jesus. <u>But the Devil—and the Satanists working for him—would like for you to lose out on heaven and have such a Rapture</u>.**

Beware Teachers of Prophecy Today— Many are Satanic Operatives

Satanists today are using Bible prophecy to push spiritual deception among Christian believers. The Rapture is <u>one</u> example of this deception. Another thing Satanists want out of the Rapture— and Bible prophecy in general—is for **Christians to be passive and non-resistant to evil.** They don't want believers to do anything to actively resist evil—as God <u>always</u> wants us to do—and which he will punish us for <u>not</u> doing. **Remember: passivity is evil.**

The Satanists want you to believe the false idea that all their evil doings in the end time are actually part of <u>God's</u> plan for the world. And if you actively resisted their evil plans, you would be in essence <u>fighting God</u>. Of course, this is false. But <u>many</u> Christians today lack discernment because they have unwittingly absorbed a fake worldview put out by the Satanic voice of the world—instead of one from God and the Bible.

Satanic operatives today are <u>actively</u> working to cause their Anti-Christ to come. They are not passive in achieving <u>their</u> agenda. Satan doesn't let them be passive. But they want Christians to stand down, do nothing and <u>passively</u> accept all their evil changes in the world.

To achieve this, Satanists place their operatives in 'Christian' media and infiltrated churches advising Christians to be <u>passive</u> so that—in doing nothing to resist evil—they will <u>cause</u> Christ to return in order to confront the forces of evil at the end time as prophesied. Christ <u>will</u> certainly return one day to do this—but won't appreciate your lack of effort for him in the meantime.

As they always do, **Satanists invert things. What is good, they say is bad—and vice-versa. Resisting evil—which is good and our duty before God—is now supposedly bad** the Satanists say—in their disguise as Bible prophecy teachers. **Doing so only <u>hinders</u> God's plans for the end time and only serves to <u>delay</u> the time of Christ's return**.

And, besides, they imply—if not outright say—why do you care what evil happens to other people at the end time? <u>You</u> are going to be OK. After all, you and all your believing family and friends are going to be magically transported to heaven by God during the Rapture—away from the mess happening down here on earth.

So—on top of their other evils—**people pushing the Rapture** and other fake Bible prophecy **are encouraging Christians to disregard the welfare of their neighbor**. This directly contradicts Jesus' command to us all in *Mark* 12:30-31 when he was asked what the greatest commandment was,

"Love the Lord your God with all your heart and with all your soul and with all your mind and with all your strength. The second is this: '**Love your neighbor as yourself**.'"

Even if the Bible prophecy pushed by a particular teacher is not so spiritually toxic as to advise passivity in the face of evil, and to put one's hopes on a coming Rapture, it is of no value to you whatsoever. Most Bible prophecy is <u>uselessly vague and speculative</u>. Or it tries to overdo it the other way: <u>linking all the allegorical and figurative language in the *Book of Revelation* with specific nations and people alive today</u>. In <u>most</u> cases—there is no clear Biblical evidence for anything they say.

You would be rich, if you had a dollar for each person in history who lived and then went to their grave that Bible prophecy 'experts' claimed—with no doubt or hesitation—was <u>the</u> much prophesied Anti-Christ.

All you need to know and care about—and which is certain—is that Christ is coming again <u>one day</u> at the end of time. Diligently <u>do</u> all the work Christ told you to do while you are waiting for him—and all will be well. But if you slack off in serving him because you are caught up in Bible prophecy lies—you may well have literal hell to pay when Jesus <u>does</u> come again.

Also Beware End-Time Christian 'Prophets'

Another type of Satanic operative inserted into the 'Christian' world today—is the so-called Christian 'prophet'. Though real prophets existed in the church in New Testament times, they didn't play a big role. Today, with much greater Satanic control of the world and its media, fake Christian prophets are making a comeback with a little help from the Devil and his friends.

First of all—don't be impressed that much of what they say <u>does</u> come true. The global Satanic power structure directs world events today—to the degree God that allows them to. Everything they do is planned out meticulously many years into the future. Since these 'prophets' are operatives working

for them—the Satanic power structure will share with them <u>in advance</u> some details of things they are about to do.

Knowing accurate details of the future is no guarantee that you are from God. **The Devil and his demons are also aware of truth— often much <u>more</u> than people are.** When Jesus came to earth, the demons were well aware that he was the Messiah and said so. Jesus had to tell them to shut up about this—so they wouldn't unduly tip people off. **Compare the demons' knowledge with that of the Jewish religious establishment—and many of the people in his hometown of Nazareth—who ignorantly thought Jesus was a <u>fraud</u>.**

You Don't Need Prophets Today Because <u>There is No New Revelation from God to Give</u>

People calling themselves 'prophets' today are obvious Satanic frauds. Satanists, as we saw, like to invert things—and they like to <u>counterfeit</u> them as well. This is because they do not have the power to <u>create</u>. So all they can do is <u>copy</u> God's creation—but always with an evil twist. True prophets of God in the Old Testament brought genuine new knowledge and revelation from God to the people of ancient Israel.

God <u>used to dwell</u> on earth with people (= ancient Israel)— but no longer does. In the same way, God <u>used to give revelation to people through prophets—but no longer does</u>. Why not? Because he has <u>already</u> said all that needs to be said. Even the New Testament doesn't tell us anything we didn't already know from the Old Testament.

You just have to know how to read the Old Testament. For example, **you have to convert literal to spiritual—as we said. The teaching of the Trinity is there in the Old Testament.** God is one— we read—in *Deuteronomy* 6:4, but the Hebrew words for 'God' and 'Lord' are plural. **The specific number of plurality is pinned down to 3—in *Genesis* 18—where it says God came to earth as <u>3 men</u>.**

The connection between the 3 men and God is not 100% explicitly stated—because it would confuse people of that time—but implied with plausible deniability. But given the totality of the evidence—with common terms referring to God being plural—we can clearly see the Trinity presented early on.

Just because singular terms for God also exist—namely, Yahweh and El—does not negate any of this. God is both 3 and 1 at the same time. So it is not a shock that you would have terms for God that are both plural <u>and</u> singular. But just having the <u>plural</u> terms for him and the <u>plural</u> imagery shows there is a <u>plurality</u> to God as well—the Trinity.

The Old Testament <u>foreshadows all the events and teachings of the New Testament</u>. The main events in Jesus' life are foretold through the Old Testament Messianic prophecies of his life. **In the book of Jonah, we see God is concerned about the spiritual welfare of the Assyrians—a people far distant from ancient Israel—and uncircumcised, non-Jews at that**.

The prophet Joel says (in *Joel* 2:28) that the Spirit of God will one day be poured out on 'all people'—not just Jews in Israel. If the Old Testament says the Chosen People are literal Israel, we know—by now—this means that **the Chosen People are really <u>spiritual</u> Israel (= Christians) who are <u>spiritually</u> circumcised** who have set themselves apart from the world to follow the one, true God of Israel.

Christians today who—foolishly—give heed to 'prophets', are just setting themselves up to be <u>deceived</u> with Satanic lies that will destroy their faith in God.

The Devil is 'a liar and the father of lies' as Jesus correctly said in *John* 8:44. But the forces of evil are happy to speak the truth if it will further their broader cause of deception. **'Christian prophets' are allowed to speak a few words of truth to build credibility with Christians. Once they have established credibility—they can then pipe a stream of Satanic lies and disinformation directly** into churches and be believed. **Speaking a little truth in return for telling many lies—is an <u>acceptable</u> trade-off for Satanists**.

And that is why you can go to some practitioner of the occult—such as a witch—to get your fortune told and what they say <u>may well be accurate</u>. The Devil can—and often does— feed some accurate information to his people. **Some people foolishly are very impressed with the minor power that evil people are given to tell the future and do minor spiritual deeds—like impose curses.** They think maybe they should join the dark side because that is where all the <u>real</u> power seems to be.

They might easily get that impression if all they know is life in a spiritually dead, crypto-satanic church of men. **But the power of good—in a real church of power—is always much <u>greater</u> than evil. And what little you get from pursuing the path of evil— comes at a steep cost.** One of the 8 groups of people destined for the Lake of Fire in Hell for eternity—if they don't repent and accept Christ—are '**those who practice magic arts'**. This is the occult or evil. (*Revelation* 21:8).

So many Christians today—and people in general—can't really have any faith in God because they have imbibed too many Satanic lies from the world. The Gospels say that Jesus began his ministry by being tempted by the Devil. But people today think they are being sophisticated and modern—by <u>not</u> believing in the Devil.

Half of Jesus' ministry was casting out demons. But people today say they don't believe in demonic possession. They don't believe in the Devil or demons and say that what we see in the Bible with demonic possession reflects simply undiagnosed mental health issues without any spiritual component to them.

If you don't believe in Jesus or the Bible—what kind of faith do you think you have? The answer is—<u>you don't have any</u>. Even in secular matters—that won't affect the survival of one's soul in the afterlife—the level of Satanic deception is great. Many people don't believe in an overarching Satanic power structure that is steering world events to Armageddon—even as events are actively moving in that very direction.

One of the <u>biggest</u> deceptions of the Satanists is to get people to believe that 'all wars are caused by religion'—especially Christianity. This despite the fact that **it is the banker-Satanists themselves who manipulate countries they control into starting wars to allow them—behind the scenes—to plunder the natural resources and wealth of each country in the world.**

Having made many millions suffer and die because of their greed, the Satanists' media machines put out the spin that their enemies—genuine religious believers—were behind everything. The general public seems to go along and believe it. It is an amazing and largely successful fraud. This is one of the benefits of having good public relations: lies can become truth.

With levels of Satanic deception running this high, you cannot—at the same time—have a flourishing, Spirit-led church. And without a strong church as a powerful counterforce to the Satanists—people's prospects for eternity are turning increasingly bleak.

People need to realize—because they don't sufficiently right now: you wouldn't drink tiny bottles of poison every day. Nor should you imbibe every day Satanic poison from the 'culture creators' in the media.

This is the Satanic spin they put into our culture. And from the culture—it then enters our heads—through their news, entertainment, education and even mainstream religion. It will create for you and your loved ones a worldview that is friendly to them—the Satanists—and hostile to God and the Bible. It will make it hard for you to accept God and imperil your eternity as a result.

This is because **when you are steeped in a Satanic worldview, everything that is good, truthful and spiritually in your eternal best interests—will seem to you to be <u>the opposite</u>: bad, false and not to be followed.** Mission accomplished! That's why they spent all that money from their usury sin to create the entire media complex of the modern world: to turn the world upside down with their standard Satanic inversion of things.

But it has been this way for <u>all</u> of human history. Only the technology and means of deception change over time. That is why <u>only 17% of people in each generation</u> manage to fight past the deception to embrace God's free gift of paradise in Living Heaven.

For Skeptics of Satanic Schemes, Paul Warns Us 2000 Years Ago to Beware Them

In *2 Corinthians* 2:11, Paul writes to the church at Corinth that he took a certain action—forgave someone,

> **"That Satan might not outwit us. For we are not unaware of his schemes."**

If So Many Churches Have Problems, What Should Believers Do?

Hebrews **10:25 tells us that believers should not give up meeting together.** But since so many churches today are toxic to our spiritual health, what should believers in America—and much of the West—do?

You should probably switch to private house churches with other like-minded believers who share your values and dedication to the faith. That way—you won't have your spiritual zeal gradually sapped over time by mainstream churches that lack the Spirit or are Satanically-infiltrated.

It <u>doesn't</u> matter whether the infiltration is great or small. Or whether the infiltration is run by many trained operatives or just a few amateurs. **Flee this Satanic spiritual pollution that will poison and suffocate the faith of you and your family.**

Having the option of **starting up a house church—means you don't have to put up with the spiritual <u>mediocrity</u> of today's churches. It also frees you from the danger to your faith of heresy that is also making its way into a number of churches today.**

It also increases the skill set of every believer. The U.S. Marine Corps believes that every marine should be a rifleman capable of fighting proficiently—regardless of their job assignment. In the same way, every believer—in the <u>spiritual</u> war between good and evil—should be able to evangelize the unsaved and set up and run a church made up of any converts they make.

In Jesus' day, the main opponents to his ministry were the <u>religious establishment</u>. They were not outside evil infiltrators into a good system. Rather, they were the entrenched rulers of an evil bureaucracy that was rotten to the core. Jesus said in *Matthew* 5:20,

> **"I tell you that unless your righteousness**
> **surpasses that of the Pharisees and**
> **the teachers of the law, you will certainly**
> **not enter the kingdom of heaven."**

When none of your religious leaders, teachers and experts in the law is going to make it into heaven—you know you have a problem. Pretty much the <u>entire</u> Jewish religious structure was headed for Hell.

Jesus was a threat to the power structure—so they arranged for his murder. Before this, Jesus had confronted them in *John* 8:44,

> **"You belong to your father, the Devil,**
> **and you want to carry out**
> **your father's desires."**

So the religious establishment in Jesus' day was evil—but the early <u>church</u> was different. **It was spirit-led, active and everyone**

held their wealth in common. You can read all about it in the *Book of Acts* in the Bible. It starts with the ascension of Jesus to heaven, the coming of the Holy Spirit on Pentecost and continues to the spread of the Gospel outside of Israel to non-Jews (= Gentiles) living in the Greco-Roman empire.

When you compare the early, dynamic Church of the 1st century to today's churches—you will notice many differences. **One difference is that today's church in general is very passive**. They go to church for an hour a week. Then they go home. There is no burden or expectation felt that they need to be witnessing to friends, neighbors and co-workers <u>every day</u>. Today's church <u>doesn't</u> evangelize much anymore. **Passivity before evil—we said--<u>is</u> evil. But passivity <u>itself</u> is evil. You are squandering precious time that could be used for things that have <u>eternal</u> consequences**. The focus today seems to be on oneself and one's family—not serving God.

To ensure a proper focus on evangelization and high spirituality—<u>the early church held all their money and possessions in common</u>. When people got money, they gave it to the church—to help the needy, fund evangelists and meet the needs of current church members.

Doing things this way ensured that the church had high spirituality. **One of the biggest limiting factors in terms of people's spirituality—is money. Any money that you privately hold onto—beyond for the basics such as food, clothing and shelter—is spiritually harmful**.

For the nature of money is such that **as your wallet grows, your heart shrinks**. Why? Because when you get money, you are able to help those around you who are in need. God will soon put it in your heart to help someone nearby you with your money. **If you resist God's overture, you will drive God away from you**—because **<u>money</u> has become your new god**. Jesus said in *Matthew* 6:24,

"You cannot serve both God and money."

Because of your idolatry with money, you will have no spiritual productivity and your heart will soon grow very cold to God. *James* 5:1-3 warns people with money—who are in this spiritual condition—about what awaits them in the future,

"Now listen, you rich people, weep and
wail because of the misery that
is coming on you. Your wealth has rotted,
and moths have eaten your
clothes. Your gold and silver are corroded. Their corrosion will
testify against you and eat your flesh
like fire. You have hoarded
wealth in the last days."

Hoarding wealth—that is, clinging to wealth beyond one's basic needs—is one of the biggest destroyers of people's souls. Only people with a Satanic agenda could possibly push a 'Prosperity Gospel' to focus people on the deadly and suicidal pursuit of accumulating earthly wealth.

Adding to the evil of it all, they sell it to Christians—who should know better—and blasphemously include the word 'Gospel' in its name. **The Gospel—meaning the 'good news' of salvation for all through Jesus—becomes in this context the opposite of this: the bad news that you are not making it to Living Heaven—because your excess wealth has killed off your soul**.

Beware Biblical Booby Traps

Biblical 'booby traps' are things that God deliberately put into the Bible that trigger people who come to God with hostility and which cause them to be deceived. If you approach God with a neutral attitude—or especially a positive one—you won't be deceived by Biblical booby traps. You might be puzzled by them and not able to fully explain them—but you won't be <u>actively misled</u> by them.

The targets of these booby traps are people with low SDF who attack God. Remember that we said: **when you sin, you bring spiritual delusion upon yourself**. Anger toward God is uninformed and brings condemnation. Rule to remember: **always practice love and humility toward God and you will receive love and blessings back.**

Here are some of the Biblical booby traps to beware:

God Was 'Walking' In the Garden of Eden

Genesis 3:8 tells us that Adam and Eve one day heard God walking in the Garden of Eden. Of course this is a figurative expression because elsewhere in the Bible—such as *Jeremiah* 23:23 it says,

"I am a God who is everywhere and not in one place only"

So if God is everywhere at the same time, how can he be limited to one place only—and who knew he had legs? This is an **anthropomorphism—or 'depiction of God with human form or attributes'**. Though it is clearly just an expression, some people will use it to dismiss any notion of God, the Bible or religion—as silly or uneducated or against reason or science.

But Wasn't Man Created in the Image of God?

Genesis 1:27 tells us, **"God created mankind in his own image"**. This means God made mankind in his own <u>spiritual</u> image <u>and</u> gave them a spiritual awareness of God and spiritual matters.

Animals—and the rest of creation—are lower creatures that <u>have</u> souls, but <u>no</u> awareness of God or spiritual matters. This benefits them, in a way. Since, as we said, they have no awareness of God—they have no guilt of sin before God. This means they will

<u>all</u> go to Living Heaven when they die—as opposed to only 17% of all 'smarter' human beings.

So God did <u>not</u> create mankind in his own <u>physical</u> image. We do not physically look like God. God is everywhere at once— mankind isn't. But our soul is made of spirit—just like God. We said that often when the language of the Old Testament is <u>literal and physical,</u> it should in fact be interpreted as <u>figurative and spiritual</u>.

This rule comes in handy in helping us properly interpret things—and we have already used it several times: **we are made in the <u>spiritual</u> image of God; <u>spiritual</u> wealth is what is good with God—not physical wealth or money; God's Chosen People are not literal Israel—who rebelled against God and were permanently banished from the Promised Land—but <u>spiritual</u> Israel (= Christians).**

But having said all this—there i<u>s</u> another way that mankind is made in the image of God. **God is triunic (= <u>3-in-1</u>) in form. God consists of the <u>Father, Son and Holy Spirit</u>.** They are 3 persons that together make up a single being or entity. **In the same way, God created mankind as triunes: each person is one being made up of three separate parts: mind, body and soul.**

For Nitpickers:

Hebrews 4:12 does <u>not</u> contradict this idea that mankind is triunic in form. There it says the Holy Spirit can pierce 'soul and spirit'. This is a mistranslation. The word here translated as 'soul' (= psyche) can also mean 'mind'. It is where we get the word psychology (= study of the mind) from.

The text should translate as 'mind and spirit (= soul). Even supporters of the current translation can offer no cogent explanation for what the difference would be between 'soul' and 'spirit'. But mankind has 3 parts like God—with no random 4th part based on a bad translation.

So—though God consists of 3 parts—they are all fully unified and function as one. That's why the Bible can speak of the Trinity in some places, but also have *Deuteronomy* 6:4 state,

"Hear, O Israel: The Lord our God, the Lord is one."

God is unified and has great power. If we—as believers in his Church—imitate God's unity, we will have much greater power and impact in whatever we do: from prayers to God, to miracles to bringing about spiritual revival in the world.

Because there is so much power in unity—the Devil fears this. He is always trying to divide believers—and people in general—to weaken them and their resistance to him. So his servants—the Satanic power structure throughout the world—always seeks to divide people along many lines: men from women, the different generations, rich and poor, people of different regions, countries, races and religions, etc. Don't be fooled: there is power in unity and whoever promotes division—promotes a Satanic agenda.

We Inherit God's 'Dissolvability into One'

Just as God is unified—having 3 parts that function as 1—so too are people who follow God. They become like him and the multiplicity of their backgrounds 'dissolves' into one. *Galatians* 3:28 informs us,

"There is neither Jew nor non-Jew, neither
slave nor free, nor is there
male and female, for you are all one in Christ Jesus."

We see the dissolvability-into-one principle in marriage as well. Anyone that comes into the presence of God and his love (because 'God is love' *1 John* 4:8) becomes one. Speaking of a married couple, *Mark* 10:8 tells us,

"And the two will become one flesh. So they are no longer two, but one flesh."

Even things—and polar opposites at that—become <u>one</u> in the presence of God's love. Seeking to maximize one's earthly wealth, makes you selfish and distant from God. But—in the presence of God's love—this is <u>not</u> the case. Let's say you seek to acquire great earthly wealth so you can then give it to the poor and needy—a very selfless act. You do this because you are 'greedy' to secure the highest position in heaven for yourself. So—in love—selfishness and selflessness become <u>one</u> and God blesses you in this endeavor.

<u>All multiplicity in the world disappears into one before God's love</u>.

Was God Unfair to Uzzah?

In *2 Samuel* 6:6, we learn about **Uzzah, an ancient Israelite priest responsible for transporting the Ark of the Covenant from place to place**. The oxen—pulling the cart that carried the Ark—stumbled. Uzzah saw that the Ark might fall out of the cart and onto the ground. Fearing this, he reached out and touched the Ark to keep it in the cart. But in so doing, **Uzzah violated God's strict command not to touch the Ark. Even though Uzzah's intentions were good, God's anger still blazed against him, and he struck Uzzah dead**.

Through the centuries, this story has troubled people because God became angry and killed a man who was merely trying to do good. Was God unfair to do this to Uzzah? The short answer to this question is no. God was <u>not</u> unfair to Uzzah. What happened to Uzzah is no different than what happened to Job when he suffered God's testing of him undeserved.

And it is no different than what happens to all of us today: he suffered an instance of Passive Spirituality. That is, undeserved

111

evil. It happens all the time. So God rewarded him with greater-value spiritual good that will accompany him in heaven for eternity.

This is what happens with all the animals that we eat for food every day or that were killed to sacrifice to God in ancient times. God compensates them for their experience with greater rewards of spiritual good. All animals are already going to Living Heaven, as it is—because they lack moral awareness. **God's grant of spiritual good just gives them a <u>higher place in heaven</u>**. Uzzah's case is the same. God will reward Uzzah with spiritual good to boost his place in heaven. So no. God was not unfair to Uzzah.

But the point of the story is <u>not Uzzah</u>. <u>It is about God and his harsh standard of absolute justice that prevails in God's spiritual world</u>. There, we said, intent doesn't matter when committing an action—only outcome. It doesn't matter if you didn't know something was a sin or if you did it accidentally. Uzzah committed a sin—touching the cart—so now he's dead.

The Ark of the Covenant was where God's presence dwelt in ancient Israel. It is like heaven in the spiritual world—God's normal home. <u>In heaven, God's rules are always this</u> harsh. One day, all of us will be there in front of God—potentially facing this harsh standard of justice. **The only way to avoid this harsh standard of judgement—is to become saved through faith in Christ. This will <u>switch you</u> from the harsh type of justice that Uzzah faced—to one more kind and gentle**. For reference—here are the 3 states you can stand before God in:

3 States of Being Toward God

1. **Pre-Law (= no knowledge of good and evil—no sin)**   **Garden of Eden**

2. **Law (= knowledge of good and evil—sin)**   **Normal life on earth**

3. **Grace (= knowledge of good and evil—no sin)**   **Return to Eden**

These states represent the spiritual progression that <u>each individual</u> goes through—and in parallel fashion—<u>all of mankind</u> collectively. As a child, we lack moral awareness of good and evil. So God does <u>not</u> charge us with any sin—just as he does with animals. So we can dwell with God in Eden—which symbolizes heaven. **All young children go to heaven—and all animals. Mankind—at the dawn of history**—was collectively in a childlike stage of spiritual evolution. They had a very limited grasp of God's laws of good and evil—so **God will judge them like young children**.

Why Did the Earliest People in *Genesis* Live So Long?

The *Book of Genesis* tells us that the earliest people on earth—basically Adam to Noah—lived very long lives. Several of them lived almost 1000 years. Why is this? Longevity was a symbol of God's favor—just like physical wealth.

The longer you lived—the greater your moral standing with God. Because the earliest people for the most part lacked an awareness of God's laws, he treated them collectively like little children who don't have any sin.

Their extraordinary lifespans reflect their basically sin-free status before God. But observe that with time, God's laws disseminate throughout the world and people become aware of good and evil. At this point, God charges them with sin and their lifespans dramatically lessen to ages we see today.

It is unclear if these early people <u>actually</u> lived such long lengths of time—or if this is purely symbolic. Probably the latter. The abstract theology we find in Paul's letter to the *Romans* about 'where there is no law, there is no sin' was probably over the heads of most people at this early period in human history.

God inspired the writer of these verses to convey the teaching that early people did not have much sin. But the writer did not

have the know-how to use Pauline theology to explain why this was. So God inspired the writer to simply say early people had long lifespans. This was a simple way to indicate they had God's favor (= were without sin) without having to give a complicated theological explanation for it.

Children—we said—are sinless as long as they have no awareness of good and evil. But as they grow up—they become aware of good and evil. At this point, God charges them with evil. They no longer automatically go to Living Heaven when they die—like young children and animals.

This is parallel to how Adam and Eve had to leave Eden when they sinned and—as a result—became aware of good and evil. **In fact, the Adam and Even story simply tells—in symbolic language— the story of <u>all people's spiritual progression</u> through the various states of being—individually and collectively.**

Jesus came to earth to die for our sins so that we could have the Garden of Eden all over again. Though we have sin because of our knowledge of good and evil—<u>through God's grace (= undeserved favor) coming from faith in Jesus—we can become sin-free in God's eyes</u>. Just like Adam and Eve in Eden. We can return to Eden. *John* 3:16 says,

> **"God so loved the world that he gave his
> one and only Son, that whoever
> believes in him shall not perish but have eternal life."**

Not all people, of course, pass through all three states of being in their life. Those who die as babies or young children— will only experience the Pre-Law state. Those who die as adults— but unsaved—will only reach the Law state. Those who make it to adulthood—and who <u>become</u> saved—will reach the state of Grace.

Mankind collectively entered the State of Law early on after receiving law codes like the Mosaic Law from God. It finally reached the State of Grace after the crucifixion of Jesus 2000 years ago. **Not all people will take advantage of this priceless gift; but mankind has reached the stage where becoming saved by grace <u>is</u> possible for us**.

Can Something <u>Be</u> a Sin—If Nobody in the Bible Calls It Sin? Yes.

In the <u>early</u> books of the Bible—in the Old Testament—when some action or behavior of a person is deemed sinful, it is usually labeled as such. But, at other times, objectionable behavior—without explanation—is <u>not</u> commented on as being sinful.

This has led some to think if the Bible doesn't <u>openly</u> condemn something, then that behavior is OK—and not a sin. As a result, a number of things in the Old Testament can be considered spiritual booby traps—especially certain incidents involving women.

Take, for example, the case of polygamy. Certain early Patriarchs and figures in the Bible had multiple wives. The Bible never condemns this practice as being wrong or inappropriate in any way.

So does this mean it is OK for a man to have multiple wives? **No. Jesus in *Matthew* 19 references the book of *Genesis* describing the first human couple—Adam and Eve. He says that the original marriage template God established involves a man and a woman where the two become one flesh. Any deviations from this—including polygamy—would be a sinful corruption of God's original template by later people and cultures.**

Something <u>Can</u> Be a Sin—Even If God Allows It in His Law

In *Matthew* 19, Jesus—right after discussing marriage—mentions divorce. He says God brought together a man and a woman and made the two into one flesh. Jesus concludes his answer by saying in verse 6,

"Therefore what God has joined together, let no one separate."

The Pharisees in the audience then ask him why the Law of Moses allows for divorce. Jesus responds in *Matthew* 19:8-9,

> **"Moses permitted you to divorce your**
> **wives because your hearts were**
> **hard. But it was not this way from the**
> **beginning. I tell you that anyone**
> **who divorces his wife, except for sexual**
> **immorality, and marries another**
> **woman commits adultery."**

Elsewhere, in *Malachi* 2:16, God says,

> **"I hate divorce"**

So we see that **the Law of Moses in the Old Testament is not always** <u>optimal</u> **(= best possible) in nature, but sometimes** <u>concessional</u> **(= sometimes makes allowances due to imperfect real-world conditions).** The Law of Moses was not perfect—like the later teachings of Jesus in the New Testament. But the Law still gave the Israelites a massive boost in their understanding of God and his ways—from what they had earlier.

But we still sometimes find morally questionable behavior among people in certain <u>early</u> stories of the Bible. Later writers would basically concede the poor morals of certain earlier periods in their history. The editorial comment you find in *Judges* 17:6 reflects this,

"In those days Israel had no king, everyone did as they saw fit."

So you are not supposed to imitate all the behavior you read about in <u>the early parts</u> of the Bible. Nor is every detail—about <u>non-spiritual</u> matters—in the early parts correct, in a modern scientific sense. **But God leaves these inappropriate or wrong details in the text because they can still serve a broader purpose of his—deceiving people who come at him with hostility—as punishment.**

God sends small opponents of his—like ordinary people who scoff at him—small delusions such as the Biblical booby traps we have been discussing. He sends big delusions to big opponents of his—such as the Devil, demons or certain people at the end time associated with the Anti-Christ. *2 Thessalonians* 2:11-12 tell us,

> **"God will send them a powerful delusion**
> **so that they believe the**
> **lie, in order that judgement may come upon all who have**
> **disbelieved the truth and delighted in wickedness."**

Even if we don't consider ourselves rebels against God or people who mock him or the Bible, we <u>all rebel against God and suffer delusion—as a result of our sin.</u>

So what is the delusion we all suffer from because of our sins against God? The <u>average person's view of God and the world is upside down</u>. It is the exact opposite of the way things <u>really</u> are—what the Bible calls 'foolishness'. Unless God guides you to have insight into things—so that you can see things right side up (= wisdom)—you will forever remain spiritually deluded.

1 Corinthians 3:19 tells us,

> **"The wisdom of this world is foolishness in God's sight."**

The 'wisdom' of this world is foolishness because it is exactly the <u>opposite</u> of reality—in spiritual terms. This is different from earthly knowledge—such as 2 + 2 = 4, grass is green and the sky is blue. One can be—and many are—very knowledgeable about earthly matters like these. But spiritual wisdom is completely different. What people who lack God (= they are of this world) think is true spiritually (= wisdom)—is, in fact, foolishness because it is upside down.

Job 5:13 describes for us God's EOF spiritual law at work punishing people for arrogance against him,

'He catches the wise in their craftiness.'"

When people's arrogance involves mocking something in the Bible, the small-scale delusion that God sends, are Biblical booby traps. But it doesn't have to only involve mockery of the Bible. Any arrogance or mockery will trigger a retaliatory delusion from God.

Don't think of this as God being petty. Rather, view it as **God being a concerned parent**. He is trying to discipline a bratty child, so it will stop doing things that will harm its prospects for heaven in the afterworld—that God is trying to give it. That bratty child is <u>all</u> of us.

Because the average person's understanding of spiritual matters is diametrically opposed to the truth—it is easy for God to punish them with deception for any arrogance on their part. **But all of us—because of even accidental or unintentional sins committed when we weren't even trying to mock God—are spiritually deluded.**

Every time you sin, you become slightly more deluded spiritually—than the moment before you sinned. Those who are unsaved—and have a lifetime of accumulated sin—are the most spiritually deluded. But even believers who slacken in their diligence and then sin—become deluded by sin.

So if you sin—you must <u>right away</u> seek immediate forgiveness by praying to God. This—done with a <u>sincere</u> heart—should restore whatever spiritual clarity you lost because of your earlier sin. But if your heart is not sincere when you pray to God, your spiritual clarity will not return, because you are <u>still</u> in your sin. You <u>didn't</u> truly repent of your sins—and God knows that—because you can't fool him. In fact, you committed another sin by lying to God about your repentance.

Do everything with a truthful and sincere heart. Also, always approach God with great humility to avoid *any* delusion—big or small.

You Can Especially See with Salvation That God 'catches the wise in their craftiness'

As we saw with the saying 'the last will be first, and the first will be last', **few of those who are wise in their own eyes or wealthy or powerful in this world will make it to Living Heaven.** Contrast this with the lowly and meek, such as animals (= lower forms of life), babies and young children who will <u>all</u> make it to Living Heaven.

Demons & Demonic Possession

Strictly speaking, the frequent mention in the Gospels of demons and demonic possession—is <u>not</u> a Biblical booby trap. That is, God did <u>not</u> put that material in the Bible <u>specifically to trip people up</u>. But it has <u>effectively</u> become a booby trap—because it is a stumbling block for many today. In the Gospels, demons are everywhere. In modern Western societies—not so much. Why is that?

The answer is twofold. **The presence of Jesus attracts more demons than would normally show up in a place—then or now.** Even in the rest of the Bible, you don't see as much demonic activity as in the Gospels with Jesus. **As part of his mission on earth, there was—in the spiritual world—a great battle of good vs. evil that was about to take place after his crucifixion. The outcome would determine the destiny of all of mankind's souls. Demons, as foot soldiers in Satan's army, were flocking to the area.**

There is <u>Always</u> a Spiritual War Going On Around Us

At any given time, there is always a spiritual war between the forces of good and evil going on around us. The closer you are to God—the more aware of it you are. The further you are from God—the less so.

A number of scenes in the Bible describe this. For example, God in *2 Kings* 19 sends Hezekiah, the king of Judah, a powerful angel that kills 185,000 of his (human) Assyrian enemy. So you have angels fighting demons in the spiritual world—and angelic forces taking part in human battles on earth as well.

The Satanic power structure around the world has made a concerted effort to secularize all the countries of the world—especially Christian countries in the West. Don't mention or have any signs of religion in the public square, including the news, schools and colleges, places of work, stores, etc. Flood the culture with sex, materialism and vapid entertainment so that people are diverted from spirituality toward lust, greed and trivial matters.

Have sports and entertainment distract people during Sabbath days on the weekend—and at other times too. Push alternative explanations—true or not—for things in the Bible. So we are told—Darwin's theory of evolution—explains mankind's origins. We don't need the Bible account in *Genesis* anymore. Likewise—secularists tell us—demons and the idea of demonic possession can <u>all</u> be explained now by psychology as manifestations of mental illness, etc.

The cumulative effect of all this busy-ness, distraction and earthly focus in our lives—contrived for us by the Satanists who created our modern culture for us—is that **we are <u>less</u> spiritual today than in previous times and cultures. So we lose spiritual** discernment from all the delusion that sets in as a consequence of our lack of spirituality.

Another reason you don't see the Devil or his demons much today, is because **the Devil doesn't need to reveal himself in secular societies—such as our own. Why not? Because his job is already done for him. People don't believe in him. If he did actually appear, it would be** <u>counterproductive</u>**. People would then be awakened to the fact that he** <u>does</u> **exist. And if the Devil exists, then very likely his counterpart God must also exist. With this realization, many people might turn to God and religion— which the Devil** <u>doesn't</u> **want.**

So the Devil doesn't make a lot of personal appearances in a culture like ours. But this is <u>not</u> the case **in cultures today where the practice of the occult—such as witchcraft or voodoo —is widespread. There the signs of diabolic activity are too common to be dismissed by skeptics.**

Even in our culture, you can find diabolic activity—if you know where to look. For example, let's say you immerse yourself in Satanism for years. You pledge your soul to the Devil and rise to the level of a high-ranking Satanic priest. And then one day you decide to just quit and walk away. Like a heroin addict leaving the drug cold turkey—you are going to have some withdrawal issues. With Satanism, that will involve a lot of diabolic activity manifesting itself as the dark side tries to keep you under its control.

A common feeling people in secular societies today have—is a 'deadening' of their soul. When you are very spiritual and in close contact with God, you feel very much alive and vigorous in your soul or spirit. The opposite happens to you when you turn away from God. You feel very empty and dead inside. This is because your soul—when burdened and weighed down by sin—<u>dies</u>.

James 1:15 tells us,

> "After [improper] desire has conceived, it gives birth to sin; and sin, when it is full-grown, gives birth to death."

Sin is inextricably connected with death—and always has been. You can die physically (= your body) and you can die spiritually (= your soul). There is a spiritual law that applies here:

'The Spirit Leads and Guides the Flesh'

What happens in someone's soul—their spirit—<u>precedes and directs what is happening in their physical body</u>. In *Genesis* 2:17, God tells Adam and Eve after he has put them in the Garden of Eden,

> "You must not eat from the tree of the
> knowledge of good and evil,
> for when you eat from it you will certainly die."

But after they both eat from this tree—in defiance of God's command—they appear to <u>still</u> be alive. God then banishes the couple from Eden and they have to live out the remainder of their lives on earth away from the presence of God.

This is the explanation: when Adam and Eve ate from the tree and sinned, <u>their souls died at that very moment</u>. Their physical bodies were still alive. But they became mortal creatures: because once your eternal soul dies, you will only live as long as your physical body holds out.

When your soul dies because of sin—you will either go to Dead Heaven or Hell. But God can change that. If you become saved, he can—and will—resurrect your soul and send you to Living Heaven. God can also resurrect your dead soul and send you to Hell forever—if that is what you deserve.

'Soul Deadening'—God's Judgement of You <u>Before</u> Judgement Day

We said that sin brings death—to your soul first, then later at some point to your physical body. So when you sin, your soul dies. **But for most people—while they are alive—<u>their souls fluctuate back and forth between life and death</u>**. How could this be? Sin brings death, but **the opposite of sin—is love**. The opposite of 'sinning against someone'—is to 'love against someone.' God is love. **Love—the genuinely selfless act of helping others because you care for them—brings life**. *1 Peter 4:8* says,

"Love covers over a multitude of sins."

Acts of love will resurrect your soul while you are still alive. If sin brought death to your soul, acts of love will revive it. Most people's lives are a mixture of love and sin. **Love for others—family, friends and God—brings life to your soul. Sin brings death. So your soul is constantly wavering between life and death.**

God continually judges us in <u>present</u> time. We people view time in 3 parts: past, present and future. God sees only one: the present—the here and now. When you sin, your soul dies and you feel hollow and empty 'inside'. When you love others, your soul literally comes alive and you feel full of life and good. In each case, **your actions—sin or love—bring immediate judgement from God.**

In societies where Satanists have the upper hand, people don't honor God or care to do good. They indulge their own selfish desires all day. Their souls are quite dead—usually continuously. Because they feel dead inside—they seek to escape this feeling by taking drugs or other stimulants to feel alive. They seek to escape this dead feeling by having adventures or experiencing wild sensations. Then they go to doctors for help. This won't work. Their illness is spiritual—not physical. They need a spiritual cure—which doctors can't help with.

You must spiritually saturate yourself with love. Love God—first and foremost. Then all those around you—family, friends and strangers. This will bring life to your soul. If you are reading this book, you are now aware of your need to find salvation through Christ. Pray the prayer for salvation at the end of this book.

Because God continuously judges people in the present—Judgement Day in the future will be a mere formality. There won't be any surprises. If you die with a dead soul—you will go either to Dead Heaven or Hell. Most people who have only a moderate level of sin, will go to Dead Heaven. For serious offenders, God will resurrect their dead soul—just to send them to Hell for eternity. If you have a living soul—and your sins have been forgiven by Jesus (see Prayer for Salvation)—you will be transported to Living Heaven for eternity.

The Transfiguration Teaches Us about Time in Our World and the Next

In the Gospels, there is a scene called the Transfiguration where Jesus—before his crucifixion—appears in spiritual form along with Moses and Elijah from the Old Testament. The two appearing with Jesus, testify to his authenticity. Moses symbolizes the Law and Elijah the prophets. Just as these two deceased individuals testify to the authenticity of Jesus, so too do the Law and the Prophets in the Bible testify to his authenticity—as Jesus says in *Luke* 24:44.

But the Transfiguration also teaches us about the nature of time. **<u>Before</u> Jesus died on the cross for all mankind's sins, Moses and Elijah appear in spiritual form (so not still in the grave awaiting Judgement Day) and <u>saved</u>.** In other words, they were <u>already</u> saved before Jesus died on the cross to save people.

From our time perspective that is split into 3 parts—past, present and future—we would say that Jesus' saving power '<u>shot backwards</u>' to include all those born before him who needed to be saved. This included Moses and Elijah. His <u>future</u> dying on the cross goes backwards into the <u>past</u> to effect the <u>present</u> Transfiguration Jesus had with Moses and Elijah. In the spiritual world—the perspective is only one continuous present. The 3 time divisions are 1.

Notice how this 3-in 1 triunic—pattern that we have seen before—appears again with God in terms of <u>time</u>. The 3 time divisions reduce to one with God.

The *Genesis* **story of Adam and Eve teaches us a lot** of things at once. **First, it tells us how salvation works.** As we saw earlier, when someone—such as a young child—does not yet possess an awareness of good and evil, God doesn't charge them with any sin. So they can go to heaven and be with him forever. The Garden of Eden symbolizes heaven. God lives there along with all the animals who also have no sin—because they don't have an awareness of good and evil. Adam and Eve were able to live in Eden until they acquired a knowledge of good and evil. Then God charged them with sin—so they could <u>no longer</u> live with God in Eden (= heaven).

The story of Adam and Eve is the spiritual story of us all. God was able to cover a lot of complicated theology through the vehicle of a short and simple metaphorical story. It took St. Paul several epistles—especially *Romans*—**and a lot of abstract theology to convey the same information. That's why God uses stories like this to convey deep spiritual ideas. People like stories—especially children and those living early on—like metaphorical children—at the dawn of human history.**

The Adam and Eve story also illustrates other things. **What is literal in the Old Testament should really be interpreted as spiritual. So when Adam and Eve died, the text means they died** <u>spiritually</u>—**in their souls—and not their** <u>physical</u> **bodies. That is why they proceeded to keep living.**

The story also illustrates the spiritual law <u>the spirit leads and guides the flesh</u>. That is, what first happens to you <u>spiritually</u>—will later happen to you <u>physically</u>. This is the 'lead' part. The spirit leads, the body follows. The spirit or soul also has the power to direct your body. In a correctly done prayer, your soul can direct the body to heal itself—and it will. And this takes us to our next and final topic of prayer.

Lesson #5

Grow Closer to God

In the prior chapter, we spoke of things to avoid so that you don't push God away and lessen your own level of spirituality. In this last chapter, **we will speak of ways to draw closer to God—as close as possible—so that you may achieve the highest levels of spirituality**.

Closely connected to growing spiritually—is developing a powerful level of prayer. This is because **you are limited in how much you can grow spiritually—if you don't use prayer <u>to help others</u>**. Not praying for others is selfish—a lack of humility—for which God will punish you and withhold his favor.

Praying With Humility

A good way to harness the indispensable power of humility—when you pray or do anything—is to ask yourself how may I best honor God by my actions. Put God front and center of all your thoughts and he will guide you how to best please him.

Honoring God includes honoring his Sabbath day of rest—the 4th of his 10 Commandments. Earlier—more devout—generations did a better job of honoring God by honoring his Sabbath. Today—it seems that all the stores are open and people treat it pretty much as just another ordinary day. This is wrong. **Not honoring this day will harm the spiritual status of an individual and nation. Conversely, honoring it—will bless both an individual and nation.**

We find many examples in the Bible of people who had powerful prayer force. They could raise the dead, heal the sick

and even alter the weather. *James* 5:17 comments on the prayer power of the prophet Elijah,

> "Elijah was a human being, even as we
> are. He prayed earnestly that
> it would not rain, and it did not rain on
> the land for three and a half
> years."

Jesus in *Matthew* **19:26** tells us with God "all things are possible" and that, with enough faith, we can—through prayer—literally move mountains. In *Matthew* 17:20 he says,

> "Truly I tell you, if you have faith as small
> as a mustard seed, you can
> say to this mountain, 'Move from here
> to there', and it will move.
> Nothing will be impossible for you."

James 5:16 adds,

> "The prayer of a righteous person is powerful and effective."

Prayer Advice from Jesus (Mark 11:24)

> "Whatever you ask for in prayer, believe
> that you have received it,
> and it will be yours."

Achieving a high level of prayer force, however, takes a lot of time and effort—and your prayers <u>can't</u> be in violation of God's will or he <u>won't</u> answer them. Several factors are key in developing your ability to pray powerfully and effectively.

Sacrifice on your part is essential. In the Old Testament, you gave a <u>literal</u> sacrifice—of an animal or some other item—in order to get something from God. As we have seen, language that is literal in the Old Testament should really be interpreted in a <u>spiritual</u> sense. **God had the Israelites do this in order to condition them to expect that <u>they had to</u> <u>give up</u> <u>something in order to get something</u> from God in prayer.**

Spiritual Mathematics & the Equations of Fate

<u>Prayer is very mathematical and a lot like accounting</u>. If you want something from God—that God values at 100 'spiritual units'—then your level of spiritual sacrifice must match. If you come up short, your prayer won't be answered—or at least not <u>right now</u>.

Some of that 100 spiritual unit value that God has set—may come from the <u>potential</u> for good that your prayer would bring about in the world. **God answers all prayers because he wants 'good' to be created as a result**. If you show faith in God as you pray for a sick relative—that is good. If your relative gets better—that too is good. If the faith of <u>both</u> you and your relative grows—because your prayer worked, that is the best of all.

All your prayers must be centered on—legitimate—<u>good</u> being created. Things you pray for that are selfish or that don't honor God or that violate his laws—won't be accepted by God.

So if your prayer has a hypothetical '100 spiritual unit' price tag—you can pay God part of that in terms of <u>Active Good</u> that you do. The rest will be covered from the good that God knows will come about in the world if he grants your prayer. This is the <u>Potential Good</u>.

Let us take a prayer God values at our hypothetical 100 spiritual units—which we are using for illustrative purposes. Maybe 50 of these units must be achieved by active good deeds. The other 50 can come from the spiritual potential for good that would result. Or some other proportion between Active Good and Potential Good.

The problem is, we don't know exactly what value God sets for any particular prayer we make. We just do our best at:

1) Doing good deeds   2) Being righteous   3) Sacrifice

Active Good consists of <u>these 3 things</u>. We know being righteous is important because *Proverbs* 15:29 tells us,

> **"The Lord is far from the wicked, but he
> hears the prayer of the righteous."**

As we do good deeds—such as giving to the poor—we won't know exactly how many spiritual units we are accruing along the way. **But when we do eventually reach the required amount of spiritual units from Active Good—good deeds, righteousness and sacrifice—God will answer our prayer.**

Something important to keep in mind when you pray for certain things—such as that people become saved—is this: God doesn't <u>force</u> people to accept his offer of salvation. So if someone is resisting becoming saved, their resistance <u>can block your prayer</u>—because God won't use force to override their stubborn resistance. So the resistance level of the people you are praying for—is a definite additional factor in play.

We saw earlier in *Matthew* 13:58 that Jesus' prayers for people in his hometown of Nazareth were being blocked by the people he prayed for. So he couldn't do many miracles there because of that. In that case, the limiting or blocking factor was a simple lack of faith that God requires of people to heal them. Whether the blocking factor is lack of faith or refusal to go along with prayed for change in their life—this is resistance to your prayers.

At the end time, unfortunately, the <u>average</u> resistance levels of the unsaved will be <u>higher</u> than at any prior time in world history. This is because Satanic world control and the deceitful programming of people toward evil—is at an all-time high. Many people with the lowest SDF levels—known before the creation of the world—were assigned by God to live in this last period of time before Armageddon. This accounts for its low overall spiritual level.

So evangelism will be difficult—and in some cases impossible. We must always try however and never give up. Some people's souls can <u>still</u> be won over. But it will take huge amounts of effort in order to overcome people's high resistance levels to God in this last period. This will include marathon bouts of prayer—especially powerful collective prayer in order to maximize the effect—as well as good deeds, sacrifice and love.

Electricity is the Material World Equivalent of Prayer

Electricity is the power to get things done in the Material World. Prayer is the power to get things done on a spiritual level. They have parallel designs. Electricity basically consists of amps, volts and ohms. Amps measure the amount of electricity flowing through a circuit. Amps are equivalent to the amount of active good you must do to get your prayer answered. Volts measure the electric potential at which electricity flows through a circuit. Volts are equivalent to the spiritual potential for good that exists with your prayer. Ohms measure the resistance to an electrical current. Ohms are equivalent to the amount of resistance that people you are praying for—exhibit.

To get our prayers to God answered—we must amass sufficient levels of Active Good. **This includes doing good deeds, being righteous overall and making sacrifices to and for God**. Good deeds include showing faith through lengthy, continual, sincere and heart-felt prayers to God. The more exertion put forth—in terms of time, effort and sacrifice—and the deeper the levels reached in one's soul while in prayer—the more powerful the impact with God.

The Importance of Sacrifice

Sacrifice is <u>essential</u> to building a high level of spiritual good with God—to use for prayers or to bolster your status in heaven. Indeed—without it—Jesus says in *Luke* 9:23 you <u>can't even be a follower of his,</u>

> **"Whoever wants to be my disciple must
> deny themselves and take up
> their cross daily and follow me."**

This saying of Jesus calls attention to the <u>central conflict that all believers face</u>: will we succeed in suppressing our desire to indulge in earthly pleasures in order to honor God and serve him? In other words, do we have faith enough to defer current earthly pleasures—while others around us are indulging themselves in them—for greater heavenly pleasures to come as rewards in the next life?

If believers can't win this war <u>within</u> themselves, they will not be able to win any spiritual battles in the world <u>outside</u> themselves. Indeed, they likely won't even make it to Living Heaven in the first place.

Modern churches—and cushy modern life in general—have not prepared us for the sacrifice often needed to succeed with God's high-value prayers. This includes personal righteousness and a disciplined spiritual life of self-denial and restraint that purges vices and excesses from our life in dedication to serving God first and foremost. Paul tells us in *1 Thessalonians* 5:16-18,

> **"Rejoice always, pray continually, give
> thanks in all circumstances;
> for this is God's will for you in Christ Jesus."**

Each thing Paul asks us to do in these verses, are expressions of faith—the only way for us to please God (*Hebrews* 11:6). **Lengthy prayer takes faith—that there is a God, that he hears prayer and that he honors our sacrifice to him—in terms of our time, effort and emotion.** Rejoicing indicates you are happy and content with the life God has given you. So you are expressing faith in his providence. **Gratitude is likewise an expression of faith, because you are asserting that God is the source of all the good in your life.**

A Life Without Adversity Is a Life Without Spiritual Power

Adversity—though unpleasant to go through—is the <u>raw material or fuel</u> that powers prayer. If we can successfully overcome adversity with faith in God and a good spirit—God counts that as a good deed. He **will convert it to spiritual money credited to our bank account.** We can then use it whenever we pray for something to help pay for the spiritual units that God requires for that prayer to be granted. And so a life without any adversity—though tempting to pray for—would actually leave us with little prayer power and little overall spiritual development—which is <u>not</u> good.

The Bible gives us general advice on what kind of life we should lead once we are saved.
James 1:27 tells us,

> **"Religion that God our Father accepts as pure and faultless is this: to look after orphans and widows in their distress and to keep oneself from being polluted by the world."**

This combines two elements of Active Good—good deeds and personal righteousness.

Paul adds more details in his advice to us in *1 Thessalonians* 5:14-15,

> **""Encourage the disheartened, help the
> weak, be patient with everyone.
> Make sure that nobody pays back wrong
> for wrong, but always strive
> to do what is good for each other and for everyone else."**

In our efforts to amass Active Good—in order to have God answer our prayers—we must take care to <u>avoid</u> 3 things in particular:

1. **Lack of forgiveness**
2. **Lack of humility (= pride)**
3. **Lack of love**

A lack of forgiveness has the power to <u>block</u> our spiritual growth before God. If we do <u>not</u> forgive others, God will not forgive us—thus preventing us from clearing away our sins. <u>The presence of unforgiven sin in us, blocks God's efforts to bless us and answer our prayers</u>. So don't expect God to answer any of your prayers—if you have unforgiveness in your heart.

The following is the classic parable of Jesus on the need to forgive in *Matthew* 18:23-35. I quote it in full—given its importance,

> "The kingdom of heaven is like a king
> who wanted to settle accounts
> with his servants. As he began the settlement, a man who owed
> him ten thousand bags of gold was brought to him. Since he was
> not able to pay, the master ordered that he and his wife and his
> children and all that he had be sold to repay the debt. At this the
> servant fell on his knees before him. 'Be
> patient with me,' he begged,

'and I will pay back everything.' The servant's master took pity on him, canceled the debt and let him go.
But when that servant went
out, he found one of his fellow servants who owed him a hundred silver coins. He grabbed him and began to choke him. 'Pay back what you owe me!' he demanded. His
fellow servant fell to his knees
and begged him, 'Be patient with me, and I will pay it back.' But he refused. Instead, he went off and had the man thrown into prison until he could pay the debt. When the
other servants saw what had
happened, they were outraged and went and told their master everything that had happened. Then the master called the servant in. 'You wicked servant,' he said, 'I canceled all that debt of yours because you begged me to. Shouldn't you have had mercy on your fellow servant just as I had on you?' In anger his master handed him over to the jailers to be
tortured, until he should pay back
all he owed. This is how my heavenly Father
will treat each of you unless
you forgive your brother or sister from your heart."

Just before this, in *Matthew* 18:21-23 we find additional information about forgiveness,

> **"Then Peter came to Jesus and asked,**
> **'Lord, how many times shall I**
> **forgive my brother or sister who sins**
> **against me? Up to seven times?'**
> **Jesus answered, 'I tell you, not seven**
> **times, but seventy-seven times.'"**

Jesus, of course, means by this that **you must forgive people an infinite number of times** because he says elsewhere in *Matthew* 6:15,

> **"If you do not forgive others their sins,**
> **your Father will not forgive**
> **your sins."**

So regardless of how many times people sin against you—77 or many more—**God <u>each</u> <u>time</u> will block the forgiveness of <u>your</u> sins—if you don't forgive others their sins first.**

Humility, as we saw earlier, is an essential virtue to develop. The lack of it—pride—will harm your relationship with God and others and must be avoided. Peter tells us in *1 Peter* 5:5,

> **"All of you, clothe yourselves with**
> **humility toward one another,**
> **because, 'God opposes the proud but**
> **shows favor to the humble."**

One way God opposes the proud—is by <u>not</u> answering their prayers. So stay humble. As we saw earlier, **when you humble yourself, God says he will lift you up—closer to him. So humility gets you closer to God. Forgiving others their sins, will get God to forgive your sins—so you have no blocks on your own spiritual growth. This is essential to getting your prayers answered.**

A third thing you must avoid when amassing Active Good—is a lack of love. This will greatly harm you spiritually. Paul tells us in *1 Corinthians* 13:2-3 that **<u>any</u> good deeds of Active Good you do, will be <u>entirely</u> negated—if you lack love,**

> **"If I have a faith that can move mountains, but do not have**
> **love, I am nothing. If I give all I possess to the poor and give**
> **over my body to hardship that I may boast, but do not have**
> **love, I gain nothing."**

So love is indispensable. Without it, you can achieve nothing spiritually. So we must look further into what love is. Paul gives a famous description of love in *1 Corinthians* 13:4-8,

"Love is patient, love is kind. It does
not envy, it does not boast, it
is not proud. It does not dishonor
others, it is not self-seeking, it
is not easily angered, it keeps no record
of wrongs. Love does not
delight in evil but rejoices with the truth.
It always protects, always
trusts, always hopes, always perseveres. Love never fails."

The simplest way to define love—that embraces all the many examples of it that Paul gives us—is this:

To Love Is 'to Elevate Someone Spiritually'

This is attending to a person's physical needs: like a mother does for her young children or someone for an elderly or disabled parent. Or helping people spiritually; pulling them away from their sins and toward God. Or giving people hope, comfort and guidance where there was none before, etc. **Doing for someone whatever elevates their status with God—is love.**

This is the broadest possible definition of love that embraces the many different forms it can assume. This is what God does for us all the time. He tends to our physical and especially our spiritual needs--since eternity lasts much longer than our physical life.

Spiritual Warfare & Prayer

As we said, **there is always continual warfare going on in the spiritual world: angels and demons fighting over the souls of the living.** Your prayers must reflect this. The Devil, his demons and people who worship the Devil—are attacking believers and ordinary people all the time by their actions in the—very real—spiritual world.

These attacks carry <u>real power</u> to hurt people or make them susceptible to being overcome by impulses to do evil. You must <u>block</u> these attacks by the forces of evil in the spiritual realm. By the same token—in your prayers—you must pray to overcome and defeat any strongholds of evil—whether they exist in an individual, a group, an institution or an entire nation—or the whole world.

The more you pray for—the higher the spiritual cost with God. So be thankful for everything that happens to you: the good things of course, but also all the adversity and temptation which—if overcome—God will convert into spiritual good which you can then use in your prayers and spiritual warfare.

In God's world—<u>everything is good</u>—as *Romans* 8:28 tells us. Good is good—and bad is also good—in the case of adversity, if it is properly handled.

Miracles <u>Are</u> Real—and Possible—In Environments of <u>High</u> Spirituality

Miracles, signs and wonders are <u>all possible in high spirituality environments—as they</u> <u>always have been</u>. Nothing has changed—either God or the circumstances under which he has the Holy Spirit work miracles.

So why don't we see any today? Several reasons. One is that you aren't looking in the right places. They are still happening today. But your source of news—likely the mainstream media—is not about to help you in your search. They are all owned by ultra-wealthy, Satanic forces who have <u>no</u> interest in telling you uplifting stories of genuine miracles—though they know about them.

But they <u>will</u> be happy to steer you to some other stories: a fake miracle worker who they are trying to pass off as real, so you will follow a heretic and be deceived; or a cynical expose of a fake miracle worker who gets caught deceiving poor and trusting souls—to discourage you about all miracles; or they will interview a professor posing as an honest theology expert—but is really one of their paid operatives (and maybe even teaching in one of the fake theological seminaries that they have set up)—who assures us that the age of miracles is long in the past.

Of course, they will never cite any evidence from the Bible for why this might be the case—because it is <u>not</u> true and <u>there is no evidence for this</u>. But they usually don't <u>need</u> any evidence because the average person gullibly accepts almost everything that comes out of the mouth of someone who the media describe as an 'expert'. So people just defer to the <u>authority</u> of someone—without ever seeking proof or evidence—as we discussed earlier in regard to macroevolution.

But this problem of trusting 'authority' over proof and evidence is much more widespread than just macroevolution and miracles. In almost every area of life—religious or non-religious—people are being deceived by the very news sources they trust. People make bad decisions in all areas of their life because they are given bad advice—<u>deliberately</u>. This includes your diet, medical care, education, politics, financial investments—<u>and especially your spiritual life</u>.

Satanists will discourage you from believing in miracles, because they want you to give up and not even try for high spirituality. Why bother trying to do miracles today—if some professor says they were only for the people in the Bible—not people in our own day? Miracles <u>still</u> occur in churches and local Christian communities all over the world today—but are usually only covered by the local religious media that we in America never hear about.

All that being said—it <u>is</u> harder to find and do miracles today. People in general have much lower spiritual levels than many prior generations that were able to perform them. Our culture has been saturated by Satanic imagery, culture and thoughts. Any evil in our lives pushes God away from us and limits our spiritual potential.

The fact that our cultures are so Satanized today makes it harder for us to get God to do miracles for us—and also for people to receive them—since they have become so resistant to God and Gospel-hardened. **That is, we are less able to generate the level of spiritual good that is necessary for a miracle, and the resistance level of the potential recipient of a miracle has also become too high. But miracles are <u>still</u> possible when someone has <u>a high enough prayer force and the recipient has a low enough resistance</u>.**

Applying Your Prayer Force

You have built yourself up spiritually—like a bodybuilder develops their physical body. You have prayed faithfully for long periods of time. You have kept yourself holy and free from sin. You have done good deeds for your neighbor—all the while avoiding things that would limit your spiritual growth: lack of forgiveness, lack of humility and lack of genuine love.

Having done all this, you have developed the power of your prayer with God. **It is now time for you to direct it somewhere. You can pray for an individual who is lost or an entire household of people. Even better—if you can do it—because it comes at a much greater spiritual price with God—is to pray for a <u>revival</u>.**

This is a powerful outpouring of the Spirit of God on an entire community that causes many to be saved. Read *Acts* 2 in the Bible about the original great outpouring of the Holy Spirit on Pentecost. Many were saved and dramatic miracles and workings of God occurred. Read also about the 1st and 2nd Great Revivals that occurred in England and America in the 18th and early 19th centuries. Many were saved and dramatic signs of God's presence were reported—such as never happen today.

After about the early 19th century, the Satanists began to stage counterfeit revivals with (their own) fake preachers and therefore with fake results. So the term 'revival' in recent times reflects this. Pretty much everything calling itself a revival in America in the 20th century or today is in some way under the auspices of the Satanists.

One way to tell if a revival is likely fake, is to note whether they call for prayer <u>and public fasting</u>. The genuine revivals of the 1700's and early 1800's would always do this. Indeed, it was common—even apart from specific revivals—for there to be calls for national repentance and fasting, if the nation was facing some danger—moral or otherwise.

Later generations had grown too soft and comfortable—and apart from God—to do prayerful fasting anymore. God, however, said this was something that should be done and was something that the genuine church had always done—when in a crisis or when praying for a great spiritual breakthrough in evangelizing.

Genuine revivals <u>have</u> taken place in other countries in this time period though—notably China and Iran.

This is because the banker-Satanists hadn't yet spiritually poisoned and corrupted our culture as much as they have today: sex and pornography, violence, drugs and secular and anti-God culture weren't anywhere near as common as they are today. Because of this, the people were still pious in general and receptive to hearing about God and his plan of salvation for us. They weren't as Gospel-hardened, sin-entrenched and resistant to God as they are today.

Though the banker Satanists—in service to their god, the Devil—have used the profits from their sin of usury to set up companies and individuals that spread corruption throughout society—there is still hope.

There will be a <u>brief</u> window of time available soon to spread the message of salvation. This will be when the Satanists—to bring us to our knees—will collapse the economy and bring chaos upon us—that they will (through the lying media they own) blame on other nations and people. People in desperation will be <u>receptive</u> to a message of hope. This is where you come in:

Share this message of hope with those around you— <u>before it is too late</u>.

Prayer for Salvation

Lord Jesus, I realize now that you love me with all your heart in spite of all the mistakes I have made in my life. I understand you only want what is best for me.

Please forgive me for all the times that I have hurt you by sinning against you. I realize what I did was wrong and I am truly sorry.

I believe you died on the cross to cleanse me of my sins before you. I believe you were raised from the dead and I accept you now into my heart as my Lord and Savior.

Please come into my life and allow me to enjoy a personal relationship with you—now and forever. Amen.

Welcome

If you just prayed this prayer now with a sincere heart, I would like to welcome you into the community of God's children! The Bible says that whenever a person becomes saved—there is rejoicing in heaven!

The most important thing you can do now is find a good local church to attend—or a faithful group of fellow believers to meet with. We explained earlier why a small group that meets as a house church may be more helpful than a standard church these days.

Either way—being supported by fellow believers—is <u>essential</u>.

You are in a spiritual war between good and evil. Wars can be scary, depressing, frustrating and full of temptations to do the wrong thing.

A spiritual support group—such as a good house church or standard church—can help you deal with all this. The people there can help you continue to grow spiritually and get to know other believers. You will face many temptations in your life to go back to old habits, ways and friends. A good spiritual support group will help keep you on the right track. It will nurture you like a mother does her newborn child.

It is also important to keep talking to God in prayer <u>all</u> the time— and at <u>all</u> times—both good and bad. Don't just ask him for help when you are in trouble. Celebrate good times with him and be grateful for them. And talk to him in just ordinary moments as well.

Tell him your joys and fears, your successes and failures in life. Ask him for strength to get by during difficult times. Thank him for the blessings he has given you. God always wants to hear from you— at any time and about any topic. Reveal your innermost thoughts and feelings to him. May God richly bless you and watch over you in all things in your walk with him!

Printed in the United States
by Baker & Taylor Publisher Services